A PROPER GENTLEMAN

A PROPER GENTLEMAN

VERNON
SCANNELL

 Robson Books

821·914
SCA

FIRST PUBLISHED IN GREAT BRITAIN IN 1977 BY
ROBSON BOOKS LTD., 28 POLAND STREET,
LONDON W1V 3DB. COPYRIGHT © 1977 VERNON
SCANNELL.

The Author acknowledges assistance from the Arts
Council of Great Britain.

Scannell, Vernon
   A proper gentleman.
   1. Scannell, Vernon – Biography 2. Poets,
   English – 20th century – Biography
   821'.9'14   PR6037.C25Z/

ISBN 0-903895-86-2

Printed and bound in Great Britain by
REDWOOD BURN LIMITED
Trowbridge & Esher

ONE

ON JULY 2ND, 1975, I received official confirmation from The Southern Arts Association that I had been awarded a Writing Fellowship for a period of nine months. I would be required to live in the 'new village' of Berinsfield in Oxfordshire, where I would be occupying a furnished flat supplied by the County Council. A few weeks earlier, I had visited the Southern Arts headquarters in Winchester and been told that the place where the writer-in-residence would live was a model village with a population of mainly middle-class, educated people, many of whom were employed at the atomic research station at Harwell. There was a flourishing Arts Centre and the resident writer would be expected to involve himself in the cultural life of the community by organizing poetry-readings, talks and discussions, and by making himself available to give whatever help and advice he could to anyone who wished to consult him about his or her own literary efforts. He would also be expected to visit schools, colleges and literary and arts societies in the county to give talks or poetry-readings, and the Association would advise those institutions which might be interested and let them know of his availability. But it was most important that the Fellow should be allowed ample time in which to get on with his own work. He would be given an allowance of two and a half thousand pounds and would not be expected to devote more than fifteen or so hours each week to his office of itinerant jongleur and resident mentor to the apprentice poets of Berinsfield and its environs. It sounded an attractive proposition.

The commencement of the Fellowship was to be marked by my giving a reading of my poems on the evening of September 25th at the Museum of Modern Art in Oxford, after which I would take up residence in Berinsfield but, through pressure of other business or pure dilatoriness, the Southern Arts Association had been unable to arrange for the furnishing of the flat; so after the inaugural reading – an agreeably vinous occasion – I spent the night at a small private hotel on the outskirts of Oxford and then returned to where I had been living in South Wales to wait for my temporary home to be made habitable.

During the next few weeks I delivered a couple of poetry-readings followed by discussions as the new Southern Arts Literary Fellow, but I had to commute from Wales, first to Pangbourne and then to Henley-on-Thames, and it was not until November 5th that I was able to move into the flat at Berinsfield. Christopher Kerr, who was then the Southern Arts Literature Officer, told me on the telephone that, on the morning of Friday, November 5th, the BBC Television 'Book Programme' would be sending a camera-crew and their 'anchor man' Robert Robinson, to visit me at the flat where they would interview me and, later in the day, they would go with me to Banbury School where I was to speak and read to the students. The BBC people, he said, were particularly interested in the local controversy about my being given a council flat.

'What controversy is that?' I asked.

Kerr's tone was off-hand: 'Oh, apparently someone complained that you jumped the housing-queue and the local paper – the *Oxford Mail,* I believe – they've printed a piece about it. Nothing to worry about. I've been in touch with the County Council and they say it's entirely their affair. They chose to have a writer-in-residence at Berinsfield and if anybody's got any objection they'll be happy to handle it.'

So, on November 5th, I loaded my old Ford van with my typewriter, some books, clothes, pots, pans and bedding, and drove to Berinsfield, which lies between Oxford and Henley, a couple of miles from Dorchester-on-Thames. At about four in the afternoon I turned off the A423 and, for the first time, entered the place that was to be my home for the next nine months or so. The sun was shining from a freshly rinsed sky and a breeze, cold and clean as spring-water, made the air tingle. Almost anywhere would have looked inviting on such a day, but Berinsfield resisted the weather's mood. A perimeter road encircled a complex of red-brick council houses and blocks of flats. I drove past a small parade of shops – a supermarket, newsagent and post-office, a launderette and ladies' hairdressers. There was a fish-and-chip shop, a small Co-operative Store and a single pub, The Berinsfield Arms. The rest of the place reminded me of a large military depot or the married quarters of a prison, and the gaol-like aspect was increased by the huddle of roofs being overlooked by what I suppose was a water-tower, but looked like the watch-tower of a prison-camp.

I found the Junior School on whose premises, I had been told, I would find John Wright, the local Youth Leader, who was looking after the keys to my flat. He was a quiet, inconspicuously bearded man who smoked a curved Sherlock Holmes pipe. He pointed out to me the Community Centre, a large blind building with no windows, which was equipped as a gymnasium, and a smaller place where members of the Youth Club met to play table-tennis and deafening pop-music on records. There was also a shack-like structure which, John told me, was the club premises for adults and contained a bar and a room for bingo and dances.

I enquired about the Arts Centre.

He looked ruefully amused. 'Arts Centre? That sounds a bit grand. We try to run a drama group and there's a local chap, Jack Norris, who's a bit of an artist. He says he'd like to start an art class. If anybody'd go. It's not easy here.'

'Where do most of the men work?'

'Work? Well, most of them – those that *do* work, that is, they've got jobs in Cowley, the Motor Works.'

'I see.' So much for the flourishing Arts Centre and the population of middle-class intellectuals that Southern Arts had promised.

'I'll take you to the flat.'

My flat was on the ground floor of a block of similar apartments opposite the pub and fish-and-chip shop. John produced the keys and we went in.

He said, 'I think they've had a bit of a job getting furniture. That little chair was given by a lady who lives in the flat directly above you. The table and those upright chairs come from the school. Oh yes, so does the chest of drawers. I don't know where the book-case came from.'

I looked round the place with some dismay. The flat consisted of a small entrance-hall, a kitchen, a fairly large living-room with a view of the pub and fish-and-chip shop on the perimeter road, a large and a small bedroom and a bathroom. Properly furnished it could have been a comfortable, though strictly utilitarian home. But it was not properly furnished. A makeshift curtain of indeterminate colour and nondescript material had been stuck up at the front windows with drawing-pins. None of the other windows, including those in the bedroom, was curtained. The floors were quite bare and the

7

electric-light bulbs were unshaded. I looked in the main bedroom. It contained a double bed. Nothing else. The smaller bedroom was completely empty of any furniture. I had felt more at home in railway waiting-rooms.

John said, 'Anything I can do? What about eating?'

I said that I felt more like drinking.

He nodded with understanding. 'All right. I'll come back later and take you to the Community Centre club. You can meet some of the members. I'll give you a chance to get settled in here. Be back in a couple of hours.'

I unloaded the van, made up my bed and arranged my books in the old glass-fronted case and my culinary gear in the kitchen. The flat did not look much more inhabited, or habitable. I had brought some instant coffee and sugar with me so I boiled a pan of water on the antique gas stove and prepared a mug of milkless, sweet, dark fluid. I lit a cigarette, sat in the one reasonably comfortable chair and felt depression settling over me like the evening mist, damp, pervasive and enervating. It was so long since I had lived by myself and I had forgotten the taste of loneliness and was no longer adept in the stratagems for combating it. Unfocused images of imperfectly remembered bed-sitting-rooms of the past merged into one bleak cell, spectral paradigm of all those cramped and unfriendly homes in the more dismal suburbs of London – Finsbury Park, Turnpike Lane, Acton, Hanwell – the less salubrious quarters of provincial cities – Leeds, Manchester, Sheffield. I was too old now for adjustments; I was unsustained by the warm promises of countless tomorrows. I had become soft and dependent. I needed familiar surroundings, comfort, people. I was glad when John Wright returned to take me to the club.

We stood at the bar-counter and drank pints of bitter. I had been introduced to the secretary and been given a form to fill in which, with my subscription of one pound, made me a member for a year. John did not seem to me to be really at ease in the place, and I found out subsequently that he rarely went there. The couple of men he exchanged a greeting with did not seem anxious to join us. I looked around. The room was not large. There were about half-a-dozen tables with four or five chairs at each and a gambling-machine stood balefully just inside the entrance to the bar. There were no pictures on the walls but plenty of notices, mainly of a proscriptive nature: 'No alcoholic beverages will be sold to any person under the age of eighteen'; 'Drinks cannot be purchased by non-members'; 'No credit allowed'; 'No cheques cashed'; 'Members must produce membership-cards on request'. The half-dozen drinkers at the bar seemed dispirited and what little conversation took place was about a dispute at one of the Oxford motor works.

I said to John, 'Tell me about Berinsfield. What kind of place is it? How did it happen?'

Berinsfield was originally called Field Farm and, in the nineteen-forties and early 'fifties, it had been a rural slum, a local eye-sore and chronic affront to the genteel inhabitants of near-by Abingdon, Dorchester and Wallingford. During the Second World War the place had been an RAF station and when, at the end of hostilities in 1945, the service personnel had moved out, leaving the camp and huts deserted, squatters quickly moved in and, by 1947, there were over one hundred-and-fifty families living there. Conditions were bad to begin with, and they did not improve. Only one hut in twenty had running hot water and only one in five a lavatory. About half were without even a cold tap. The men of this anarchic and wildly heterogeneous community worked mainly at the car factories in Cowley, though there were a few lorry-drivers and general labourers and a handful of rag-and-bone merchants. And there were, of course, a few who had no legal occupation of any kind. Poverty and privation were severe, even among the relatively more affluent. In the ultra-respectable villages and small towns in the area Field Farm had a reputation for violence and more sinister, nameless anti-social activities were hinted at.

Berinsfield was built to accommodate these people and others who were in desperate need of proper housing, families living in over-crowded conditions with perhaps resentful relatives; some lived in condemned dwellings or were to be evicted from tied cottages; a few came from other hutted camps similar to Field Farm or were families who had been living in cramped and inadequately equipped caravans. When, in the late nineteen-fifties, the 'new village' was completed and its population moved in, the families from Field Farm were known as 'locals' and those from elsewhere as 'strangers' so, from

9

Berinsfield's earliest days, there was no sense of identity among its inhabitants and there was little hope that an integrated community would ever develop.

In the eighteen years or so of its existence the village had acquired its church, an infant and junior school, shops, post-office, community centre and health centre, but there was virtually no sign of a sense of identity as a village, no local pride. In fact many of the residents were openly and profanely derisive in their references to the place or obliquely apologetic and half-heartedly defensive. This 'new village' was – or so it seemed to many from both within and outside – a kind of ghetto for the displaced, the disreputable and defeated, a social limbo, and it was here that I had come as an apostle of sweetness and light, a cultural missionary in an unlettered jungle of red brick, bingo and booze. I would probably be eaten.

We stayed in the bar until closing-time. John was concerned about my not eating anything and he went out for fish and chips, but what appetite I might ordinarily have been feeling had by then been swamped by beer and foreboding. At ten-thirty I went back to the flat. The sour light from the unshaded electric bulbs did not make my home look any more inviting than when last seen, but dejection was now softened by drowsiness and I undressed in the dark, stumbled into bed and fell instantly asleep.

I was awakened summarily by a loud banging on the door to the flat. For a few panicky moments I had no idea where I was; then I remembered. I peered blearily at my watch and saw that it was ten minutes past nine. The banging on the door was repeated, louder still. I got out of bed, very conscious of the bare window, pulled on my old dressing-gown, and went to see who craved audience at this unsociable hour. On my way I suddenly remembered. 'Christ!' I thought, 'it's the television people! They said nine-thirty. They must be early.'

I opened the door. Three women stood there: one was big and stout with a head-scarf over curlers which made her look as if she was electrically wired for some purpose; the other two were smaller, thinner, nondescript. I regarded them with gummy eyes and said, 'Good morning.'

The big woman did the talking. 'You the poet?' she

demanded, making the word poet' sound like and insult. She spat it out as if it had a bad taste.

I mumbled some kind of admission.

The three of them advanced and I stood back to let them into the flat. In the living-room they looked round at the bare and shabby furnishings with curiosity and, I thought, a good deal of disdain.

I said, 'Look, I'm afraid I've got to get dressed. Have a shave. I'm expecting –'

The big woman cut in: 'What do you mean by moving in here? Just you. Just the one of you. This is a double flat, this is, and there's families waiting. There's a couple with a young baby. They've got to live with her mum and dad. Five of 'em in a *single* flat. And here's you in a double. What you got to say about that then?'

I felt vaguely guilty yet peevishly victimized.

'I don't know anything about your housing problems,' I said. 'I wasn't told anything about other people needing the flat. The council invited me through the Southern Arts Association. It's them you should be after, not me. If I'm robbing a family of a home I'll get out straight away. Anybody's welcome to the place. Now, I really must get dressed. Excuse me.'

I took my clothes into the bathroom and locked myself in. I ran the bath and shaved while I was sitting in the tub. For a few minutes I could hear the women talking in my living-room and then there was the sound of the outer door slamming shut and I gathered they must have left.

As I was towelling myself there was another knocking at the door. It was repeated twice, each time louder, as I finished drying and put on my dressing-gown again and went back into the hall. Again I opened my front door. A young man smiled affably. 'Hullo,' he said, 'I'm Martin Bell from the BBC 'Book Programme'. Hope I'm not too early for you.'

I asked him inside and told him I would get dressed as quickly as I could.

'No hurry. We've got to fix up the lights and mike in here. You don't mind if we start right away?'

I didn't mind. As I was dressing I heard his voice and other men's voices and the sound of things being dragged across the floor. A few minutes later, dressed and feeling slightly less hung-over, I joined Mr Bell in the living-room where he in-

11

troduced me to the camera crew who were busily trailing wires and trundling apparatus about the place.

'Robert Robinson will be here any moment. We'd like to do an interview over here by the window. Nice and relaxed. Maybe you could lean or sit on the window-sill. He'll just ask you a few questions. What do you consider your function here to be? That kind of thing. Then we'll take the cameras out into the street and film a bit of you walking around. Maybe we'll stop one or two people and ask them how they feel about having their own resident poet. Okay? Oh yes, I understand you're going to give a reading at Banbury School this afternoon. We've been in touch with the Headmaster and he's quite agreeable for us to go and film you in action. That sound okay? – Ah, here's Robert.'

I was longing for a cup of coffee, but I possessed only one mug, and I lacked the courage or thick skin to make a drink just for myself and consume it before the eyes of those men who had obviously travelled early that morning from various parts of London and were probably as much in need of refreshment as I. So I lit a cigarette, that tasted like smouldering socks, and prayed that the ordeal by camera and inquisitor would soon be over.

Robinson was amiable, intelligent and most certainly articulate, though I found his unrelenting levity a bit hard to take at that hour in the morning. The interview lasted only about ten minutes and then we all went out of the flat and a few shots were taken of me walking up and down the street. The BBC van and the cameras attracted the attention of the housewives who were shopping in the Co-op and soon a group had gathered round Robinson and me, one of whom was the large lady who had led the lynching-party which had visited my flat earlier.

She shouted to Robinson: 'Ask him why he's got a council flat when there's families as needs one! Ask him that!'

I guessed that this was just the sort of thing Robinson and the producer wanted.

Attention turned to me. 'How do you feel about this?' Robinson said. 'It *is* rather large for one person.'

I said, 'I'd no idea I was taking anybody's place in the queue for housing. If I'd known I certainly wouldn't have come. And I'm quite ready to leave, as I've already told this lady.'

Robinson evidently decided that it would not be fruitful to pursue this topic. He turned to another shopper and said, 'How

12

do you feel about having a poet in your community, your own local bard?'

She looked perplexed and nervous. 'Don't know really. All right, I suppose. Can't say I've thought much about it.'

'Well, now you've seen Vernon Scannell, do you think he looks like a poet?'

The answer came without hesitation. She shook her head vigorously. 'No. No, he don't.'

'You don't think he does? Well, what do you think poets look like then?'

Again the lady spoke with confidence. 'They're dirty,' she said, 'and they've got beards and scruffy clothes.'

'And he doesn't strike you as being like that?'

'Oh no.' She paused for a moment's reflection. 'No. He looks like a proper gentleman.' She nodded agreement with her own verdict.

Robinson was clearly delighted. This was just the kind of thing he had hoped for.

The producer was pleased, too. He said, 'Okay. I think that'll do for now.' He turned to me. 'Thanks very much. We're going to take a few shots of the village and we'll see you at Banbury this afternoon. Right?'

Right.

I went back into the flat. At last I could have that cup of coffee before driving to Banbury for lunch at the school, and the afternoon session of reading and talking to the children and answering questions.

The visit to Banbury, from my point of view and – unless they were being excessively polite – from the point of view of my hosts, was a considerable success. The television people filmed only the opening few minutes of my address and, once their distracting presence had been removed, my audience listened with gratifying attention and, when the time came for discussion, the children showed no inhibitions about asking questions, many of which showed intelligence and a lively curiosity about the nature and making of poetry. The English teaching-staff, too, were enthusiastic and well-informed and I thought the parents and children in the district were lucky to have such a school.

I arrived back in Berinsfield at about seven in the evening and found that my flat was even less welcoming than my gloomy anticipation had prepared me for. I sat down in the living-room and lit a cigarette. I sat smoking and the room and I scowled at each other for a few minutes and then I went out and crossed the road to The Berinsfield Arms. There were no other customers in the saloon but I could hear voices and the pounding beat of a juke-box from the public-bar.

The landlord was reading his evening paper and he took his time about finishing whatever item of news was engaging his interest before he asked me what I wanted to drink. He was dark and bearded, vaguely resentful-looking, and he had one of those hard, challenging stares that seem to invite charges of mendacity.

When I had taken a drink of my bitter he said, 'You the writer chap?' He spoke with a strong Lancashire accent.

I admitted it.

'Aye, read you was coming in the *Mail*. What do you think of it then?'

'Berinsfield? I haven't seen much of it yet.'

'No, and you don't want to neither.'

'Oh?'

'A terrible place. You'll see. Terrible.'

'In what way?'

He glared as if I were deliberately baiting him. 'What way? Every way! You ask anybody about these parts. You've only got to say Berinsfield and they'll run. Half the blokes here been inside. You know what I mean. Been in prison. I could point you out any night in the other bar four or five of 'em that's done time. You're not going to like it here, I can tell you. It's a right dump. Worst place I've ever been, and I've seen a few. Layabouts, villains, jailbirds, prostitutes, the lot. I tell you, it's the roughest spot I've been in and I've been in some rough places. Ten years in the Navy I was. I've been around.'

He went back to his newspaper and I finished my drink and left. I though I might return to the flat and go to bed with a book. Then I remembered the naked windows. Obviously I would have to get curtains put up before I could read in bed. There was nothing for it but to try the Community Centre bar. Perhaps John Wright would be there. In any event it could scarcely be more cheerless than the pub.

John was not there but the bar was busier than it had been at the same time on the previous evening. There must have been a dozen or so drinkers sitting at the tables and there were nine or ten standing at the bar-counter. None greeted me. I ordered my drink and remained standing there.

I don't think there was any physical movement away from me but I experienced a strong sense of the other drinkers withdrawing, a kind of metaphysical shrinking away. It was not that I was ignored. I was not. I was being watched, but covertly, shiftily almost, with barely concealed suspicion, even with something very like apprehension, and suddenly I knew what it must feel like to be one of those well-intentioned but misguided clergymen who, to show that they are fallibly human and essentially no different from their flock, blunder into the local pub and order their pints just like Charlie, Bill and Fred, only to find that their presence has cut off the flow of conversation and their own overtures are received with shifty embarrassment, sheepish grins and strangled monosyllables.

I felt myself protesting – silently, of course – to the men in the bar: Hell, what's wrong with you? I'm not what you think I am, whatever that might be. I'm not posh. I'm not one of 'them'. I left school at fourteen. I lived in a slum and I know what it's like to go hungry. I never owned a pair of pyjamas until I was twenty. I've been in the Army, a squaddie, not a bloody officer. I've done detention, I've been in the nick. I've done solitary, PD 1 – Punishment Diet Number One. I don't want to get at you, I don't want converts. I don't give a fart if you've never read a line of poetry in your life and don't want to. Suits me fine. I'm no different from you.

But they knew better, and they were right. I was different. I looked different and I sounded different. Few of my concerns were theirs, or theirs mine. If they were ever moved by verbal art it would be by the sentimentalities or stridencies of ersatz poetry, the greeting-card verse, the crude pastiche of Robert Service or the windy bombast and rant of the oligarch. Their music would offend my ears as mine would theirs. And even if we met on what might seem to be common ground, if, for instance, we talked of boxing we would still be unable properly to communicate, for what I found fascinating in the game would not in any conscious, discussable way, be of interest to them and, besides, the plummy, classy voice that I'd somehow acquired over the years would disqualify me instantly. Maybe

15

I, too, looked shifty, uneasy, apprehensive.

I decided to have one more drink and leave. The barman was drawing the pint when a voice at my side said, 'Excuse me, are you Vernon Scannell, the poet?'

The man who spoke was small, lean, and he wore a short grizzled beard and glasses, behind which his eyes looked shrewd and friendly.

I felt a great sense of relief and gratitude at being approached amicably. 'That's right,' I said. 'Have a drink.'

'No, I've got one over there. Come and join us.' He nodded towards a place at the other end of the bar where he had been drinking with a bigger man who was dressed conventionally in a dark suit and sober tie. He was drinking Guinness.

I collected my drink and followed my new companion.

He said, 'My name's Jack Norris and this is Brendan Corrigan.' The other man nodded with some of the watchfulness I had felt all around me.

Jack said, 'Actually I wrote to you the other day. Sent the letter care of the Southern Arts. They'll be sending it on to you I expect.'

I suddenly remembered John Wright talking of the local painter who was going to begin an art class. I said, 'I think someone mentioned you. Aren't you a painter?'

He look please by the description. 'Well, yes, I am really. But what I wrote to you about was a book I've written. I'd like you to have a look at it, see if it's any good. It's about the Fair Rosamond.' He looked at me with a strange mixture of interrogation, doubt and hopefulness. 'You know anything about her? The Fair Rosamond?'

'Not much. Wasn't she supposed to be Henry II's mistress?'

He looked delighted. 'That's right! She's buried at Godstow Abbey. It's believed she was murdered by the Queen Eleanor. Poisoned.'

Jack's friend said, 'They tell me you was a pro fighter.' His accent was as Irish as his name. I thought he looked sceptical.

'I was. For a short time.'

'Used to do a bit myself. Amateur.'

Jack said, 'Brendan's son's a boxer, too.'

'He is, and he's a good 'un,' Brendan said. 'He'll go a long way in the ABA's this year. He's a fighter. Keeps coming at you. Like I used to.'

16

'Where does he train?'

Brendan's expression showed disgust. 'There's a club here at the Centre. Supposed to be. It's no good though. No organization. No committee. Just one man runs it. The other night, training night, he didn't turn up, did he. What's the use of that? Kids all there, stripped off and waiting and your man never came. He thinks he can do the lot – trainer, secretary, competitions, all of it. And he ends up making a balls-up of everything. You've got to have organization. You can't run a proper club without it.'

I agreed.

Jack said, 'And how do you think you're going to like it here?'

'I haven't seen much of it yet.'

'It's all right. Not as bad as they say, I've been here a few years now. It suits me for the time being.'

'Are you a free-lance?'

'No, I work near Oxford, technical drawing, an aircraft factory. But painting and sketching's my thing.'

'John Wright tells me you're going to start an art class here.'

'That's right. I've been trying to get old Brendan to join.'

'The missus wouldn't let me,' his friend said. 'All those naked women. That's what Jack's after. The sketching's just an excuse to get the clothes off their backs.'

'And their fronts,' Jack said.

We had two or three more drinks and I went back to the flat feeling more cheerful than when I had left it. I decided that I would telephone the Southern Arts people the next day and demand more adequate furnishings. Perhaps, if the flat was made more comfortable, my nine months' stay in Berinsfield might not be too bad. At least I had met two people tonight who were reasonably congenial. Brendan, who at first had seemed to be reserving judgement on me, had become more friendly as we talked more about boxing, and before I left the club he invited me to go with him to the next training session to see his son, Mel, work out and, later in the season, we would go together to a proper show and watch the boy in serious competitive action. Jack had been entirely welcoming from the start and had been excited and pleased to talk to someone who he thought – with less than complete justification – shared his enthusiasm for the collecting rather than the reading of first editions, Sunday painting and the Fair Rosamond.

17

The following evening, a Friday, I was to give a reading at Fitzharry's School in Abingdon and on the Saturday I was off to London to spend the weekend with my friend, Peter Porter, who had just returned from a visit to the United States and whom I had not seen for two or three months. The evenings of the coming week were reserved for poetry-readings, one at Reading University and the others at various Oxfordshire schools, so I would not see Jack or Brendan for at least a week.

I undressed and got into bed, but I could not sleep. I had drunk unwisely that night: enough to stimulate, not sedate. I felt wide awake, slightly tense, vaguely endangered. What I needed, I thought, was somebody by my side in whose assuaging warmth I could for a few hours lose myself. The reluctant celibacy of the displaced was something else I must learn to contend with or, rather, something I must re-learn, for it was not a wholly unfamiliar problem. I grinned in the darkness, remembering the landlord of The Berinsfield Arms and his opprobrious references to 'jailbirds'. How would he have reacted, I wondered, if he had been told that, with my arrival in the community, the number of ex-convicts had been increased by one.

It was in 1967 that I was sent to prison for three months after pleading guilty to the charge of driving under the influence of drink. I do not wish to suggest that I regard the sentence in any absolute sense as unjustly harsh but, compared with the penalties meted out for similar and, I would have thought, more serious motoring offences, it did seem, and still does seem, disproportionate.

The circumstances of my arrest were like this: it was winter, the beginning of February, and I had driven from where I was living in Limpsfield, Surrey, to Guildford where, with Kingsley Amis and Edwin Brock, I took part in a poetry-reading. Early in the evening the weather had been unfriendly, cold, damp and misty and, by the time the reading was over, and I was preparing to drive home, a thick fog commanded the night.

In the audience was a man called Prosper Dowden, whom Edwin Brock and I both knew, and he suggested to us that we should go to his house, which was only a couple of miles away, spend the night there and continue on our way the next morning when, in all likelihood, the fog would be less hazardous or even dispersed completely. We accepted the invitation and when we arrived at Prosper's house he told us that he had given a party on the previous evening and that many bottles had been left unopened. Perhaps we should sample some. We did. We must have drunk a great deal for it was almost dawn before I crawled into bed.

The next morning I felt very unwell. I arose some time after ten o'clock and although Mrs Dowden offered me breakfast I could face nothing more demanding on the digestion than a cup of coffee. Prosper and Edwin, both of whom worked as copy-writers in a London advertising agency, had pluckily left for their offices and I sat for a while talking to Mrs Dowden and trying to summon up the energy to leave. It was about noon when I finally got away and as soon as I started to drive I realized that my hangover was going to grow even worse before it abated. My throat and mouth were parched, pain pierced my skull and eyes before which floated intangible things like little tadpoles in a murky stream. Foolishly I decided to stop at the first pub I came to and have a reviving drink, the dubiously restorative 'hair of the dog'. I told myself, quite wrongly as events were to prove, that a couple of drinks could make me feel no worse than I was already feeling and it was just possible that they might make me feel better. I drank two pints of bitter. I left the pub and got into the car and drove out of the car park. At once I knew that I was in no condition to be driving.

I had not taken into account the vast quantity of wine that I had consumed and that it was still active in my blood-stream. This was the worst kind of intoxication: aching, sick, blurring, not only lacking the least glimmer of euphoria but heavily depressing. I knew that there was only one thing to do and that was stop the car and have a sleep. Perhaps I would feel more capable after a couple of hours' rest. I drove very carefully along the quiet country road until I came to a turning into what seemed to be an ideal backwater for my siesta. The road was a cul-de-sac with solidly respectable houses and well-tended gardens on either side. I stopped the car, switched off the engine and tried to wriggle into a position comfortable enough for sleep. Just as I was dozing off I was startled by a sharp tapping on the driving-side window.

My head jerked up as if I had taken a jolting uppercut and I peered out of the car to see a middle-aged man whose mouth was opening and closing inaudibly and who, for some reason, looked very angry. I lowered the window.

'What are you doing here?' he demanded. 'You can't park here. This is a private road.'

I told him I didn't care what kind of road it was, I was staying.

Eyes and lips went suddenly narrow with suspicion. 'What do you mean, you're staying? What's wrong with you? Are you ill?'

'I'm pissed,' I said with more frankness than good sense.

For a moment he looked incredulous, then grim. 'You'd better give me your keys.'

I handed him the car-keys and he disappeared into one of the houses.

I remember thinking that, although he seemed a pompous little sod, he had really behaved quite sensibly in taking charge of the keys. Presumably he would return them once he – or both of us – decided I was fit enough to drive.

I wound up the window and settled down again for sleep. It came with merciful rapidity only to be shattered once again by banging on the car window. Painfully I dragged myself into wakefulness, opened reluctant eyes and peered out of the car. A uniformed policeman stood there with the guardian of my keys by his side. Half an hour later I was in the police station.

The police were not unpleasant. They sent for a doctor who put me through the various tests for insobriety that were customary before the introduction of the breathalyzer. I was formally charged with 'driving under the influence of drink or drugs' and the desk-sergeant allowed me to telephone my hosts of the previous night; it was arranged that I should stay with them, leaving my car, which the police had driven to the station, to be collected the next morning. I then made another call to my wife to tell her what had happened. I felt self-disgust added to the physical nausea of the hangover. It was not a happy day.

A couple of weeks later I pleaded guilty at Guildford Crown Court and was sentenced, not without some relish, I thought, by a lady magistrate, to three months' imprisonment. Then I was taken to the cells below the court to await transport to Brixton Gaol. My solicitor came down to see me.

'You could appeal,' he said. 'You might get off with a fine.'

And he would collect more money in fees: there was no 'might' about that.

I told him I would accept the court's verdict and he shrugged, without much show of concern, and went away. I sat on the wooden bed in the dim, malodorous cell and waited to be collected.

I felt a numbing sense of resignation but little or no resentment. There was, perhaps, something a shade masochistic in my acceptance: I felt that, if I did not deserve the punishment for this particular offence, then I had certainly earned it for other misdemeanours, though not necessarily of a legal nature. My chief concern was for my wife, Jo, who was eight months pregnant with our fifth child, but I knew that little disasters of this kind always summoned up reserves of fortitude and defiance in her and that, though the first shock would be followed by various problems, social and economic, she would survive without too much distress. She had friends and relatives near at hand all of whom would help in any way that was needed.

A couple of hours later my cell was unlocked and I was driven to Brixton Prison. At the forbidding portals I was handed over to a prison-officer and introduced to the processes of 'reception' which meant that I, along with twenty or so other malefactors who had been brought from other courts, was searched, stripped, weighed, medically examined, bathed and issued with prison uniform, a grey tunic and trousers, striped shirt and a pair of enormous boots, at least a couple of sizes too large for me. We were treated with a bored and brutal contempt.

Later I was locked in my cell which was furnished with a bed, table and chair, a wash-stand with a bowl and jug, and a piss-pot. Already the prison stench was beginning to seep into me, into my clothes, my hair, the pores of my skin. I could taste it sickeningly on palate and in throat. It was an impalpable stew of urine, excrement, disinfectant and something indefinable – unclean bodies and feet, no doubt, but something metaphysical, the odour of misery and hopelessness, the smell of captivity. I sat on the bed, aware of the Judas-hole in the door, and told myself I was getting too old for this kind of lark. I suspected I would not get much sleep that night and I proved to be dismally right.

21

The next morning each new convict was interviewed by one of the deputy-governors, the Governor himself being, like God, omnipotent but invisible. The young man before whom I was marched by a prison-officer was, unlike some of his colleagues, quite affable. He tapped a copy of *The Guardian* which lay on his desk. 'Been reading about you here. Seems a rather stiff sentence for drunken driving but that's not my business. The thing is what to do with you now you're here. You're in a cell on your own, aren't you?'

I said that I was.

'Well, you're lucky there. We're desperately overcrowded, up to three in a cell meant for just one man. Not very pleasant for them, but there's nothing we can do about it.'

I said, 'Is there any chance of anybody being moved into my cell?' The prospect appalled.

'Can't promise. But I think there's quite a good chance of getting you transferred to an open prison.'

'An open prison?'

'Yes. First offenders, chaps we think we can trust, we try and get them away from here.'

'What's an open prison exactly?'

'Well, you'd find it's much better than this place. You're not in cells for a start. You sleep in dormitories and you get much better facilities for recreation – there's television and football for instance.'

Dormitories, television and football! My God, I thought, I'd rather be sent to Devil's Island.

I said, 'If there's a good chance of staying in a cell on my own I think I'd rather stay here.'

His eyebrows rose. 'Really? Why?'

'I'm a bit old for football. Never was too keen on it anyway and I can't say I miss television.'

'I see...' his fingers drummed on the desk. 'Well, I can't promise anything about the cell but I'll do my best to see you're left on your own. Now, the next thing is work. Every man has to do a job of some kind or other. The library seems to be the obvious one for you. The snag is we can't simply boot the present librarian out of his job.' He looked at the officer who had escorted me into his presence and was now standing to attention by the door. 'Do you know how much longer the librarian's got to do?'

22

'No, sir, not for sure. But I don't think he's got much longer.'

'Right.' He turned his attention back to me. 'Very well. To start with you'll have to do whatever job you're given. Then as soon as the librarian's job is open you can take it over. That's the best I can do for you.'

I thanked him and I was marched out of his office.

For the next two weeks I was landing-cleaner which meant that I spent my days scrubbing and polishing floors and, more unpleasantly, attempting the Sisyphean labour of cleaning the 'recess'. The cells were on three levels and each landing had a place known as the 'recess' where every morning, when the cells were unlocked, the convicts trooped from their quarters to 'slop out'. The piss and shit from their pots was tipped into a kind of trough, the outlet of which soon became blocked so that it overflowed. It was my task to get this trough and the whole swamped area as clean as possible for the next morning's assault. I was unutterably relieved when the convict in charge of the library was discharged from prison and I took over his job.

Prison life held few surprises. Most of the prison officers were ordinary, not very intelligent, men doing an unenviable job conscientiously, usually careful to treat every prisoner with the same impersonal fairness, showing neither sympathy nor hostility. There was one, and one only, who behaved with more humanity: when it was his turn to unlock the cells at the start of the day or 'bang up' the convicts for the night he would always extend a cordial 'good morning' or 'good night' and I knew I was not alone in feeling grateful for this small recognition of our being human. Then there were two or three 'screws' who were actively unpleasant, deliberately offensive in speech and manner and constantly on the look-out for an excuse to cause trouble, cunningly and sadistically provocative, hoping to incite an act of rebellion that would give an excuse for violent retaliation.

The convicts were, naturally, a mixed lot. There were quite a few old lags, recidivists for whom prison-life was the norm; a number of small-time semi-professional criminals of all ages, a few middle-class embezzlers, a couple of ex-policemen, some drug-addicts, most of whom were segregated in the hospital wing, and a dozen or so 'hard cases' who were inside for committing GBH (Grievous Bodily Harm), robbery with violence or some similar act of mayhem. An unwritten law operated, as it does, I believe, in all prisons, which forbade anyone to ask another inmate what he was inside for; but it was quite common for a convict to volunteer this information, and many did so, either boastfully to impress, or petulantly to gain sympathy for themselves as victims of injustice.

For most of the prisoners the weekends were especially tedious because they were locked up in their cells from noon on Saturday until Monday morning with brief intervals of release only for attending church and for the daily period of exercise when we plodded slowly round the prison yard watched by bored screws. On one Sunday afternoon I was parading with the other convicts, tramping with slow mechanical tread, when there was a sudden commotion behind me, some thudding noises and cries of fear and pain. I looked round and saw that half-a-dozen convicts had set upon another, knocked him to the ground where they were busily kicking him in various parts of his body.

Whistles squealed and the screws began to shout: 'Stop that, you men! Leave that man alone! That's enough! Get marching! Go on, get moving on!'

Without any display of urgency the officers moved towards the fallen man while his assailants, after a last kick or two, resumed their slow circling of the yard, glancing back over their shoulders with self-congratulatory grins to see the officers gather round the still form of their victim, lift him to his feet and half-drag and half-carry him into the building. I recognized the injured man as a recent arrival at the prison. He was slightly-built, elderly, grey and wispy, with a white wire of a deaf-aid trailing from one ear.

I said to one of my fellow-prisoners, 'What was that about?'

'Sex-offender, I expect. They always get a doing-over. Serves him right, the dirty old sod.'

Later I learned that incidents of this kind were not uncommon. On the arrival of a new prisoner who had been convicted for a sexual crime such as rape or, more especially, the sexual assault of a child, the news quickly reached the other convicts and this release of information that was normally kept closely secret could come only from an official who had access to the documents of admission. It was noticeable that, when the screws broke up the attack on the man with the deaf-aid, they did so in a leisurely way that allowed plenty of painful damage to be inflicted before rescue was effected. It was also noticeable that they made no attempt to identify or take any kind of disciplinary action against the attackers. Here, then, was another unwritten paragraph in the unofficial penal code and I found it a disturbing one.

Apart from the beating up of the little man in the exercise yard I actually witnessed during my stay in Brixton only one other exhibition of violence and that occurred one morning at slopping-out time when one convict hit another with a pretty powerful left and right that spreadeagled him into the hideous effluent of the recess floor. I heard later that the man who had been attacked was suspected of 'grassing' or supplying information to the screws about his cell-mates' illicit activities, most probably connected with trafficking in 'snout' (the prisoners' word for tobacco). On another occasion an officer was attacked but I was not present when this event took place though I did see the splendid black eye that he sustained, a sight that gave me some pleasure for he was one of the two screws who had done their best to make life more unpleasant for me than it need have been.

No, I saw little violence, yet its threat was never absent, its presence thickening the air like the charged atmosphere before a storm. I suspected that the savage and self-righteous beating handed out to the 'sex-offender' was permitted (though not officially) at least partly to provide a quasi-honourable release for the impulse to smash and hurt that would otherwise have expressed itself in ways more alarming to the authorities.

I served two months in Brixton, the statutory month being remitted for 'good behviour'. It seemed a lot longer. Although, of course, I consumed no alcohol during that time, I felt no physical benefit. In fact for the whole of my stay I was chronically but undiagnosably unwell. The food, while sufficient in quantity, consisted of stodgy carbohydrates the very sight and smell of which was enough to murder all but the most indiscriminate appetite. I suffered from a permanent headache and there was a constant vile taste in my mouth, the taste of the smell of the place, and I could neither sleep nor concentrate for any sustained length of time. Brixton was a very good place to get out of.

TWO

I DID NOT SEE MUCH of Berinsfield and its inhabitants over the next week or so. Immediately after my pleasant weekend with Peter Porter I took part on the Monday morning in a live radio broadcast of a programme called 'Start the Week'. It was the day before the official commemoration of the 1918 Armistice and, for this reason I suppose, the topic to be discussed was war and peace. In the studio were some professional broadcasters, including Kenneth Robinson, Joan Bakewell and another lady whose name I did not catch, and it was their task to question and stimulate discussion between the guests who were Lord Soper, the nonconformist cleric and uncompromising champion of pacificism, Frederick Forsyth, the author of some popular and violent novels including *The Day of the Jackal* and *The Odessa File,* and a television producer who had recently made a film about the Second World War. I was there because I had just published a new collection of poems, *The Loving Game,* in which the themes of war and violence were touched upon, and perhaps because my own attitude to the subject was, and still is, far more equivocal than either Lord Soper's absolute refusal to countenance the moral permissibility of war under any circumstances whatsoever and Forsyth's adulation of martial prowess. 'Man,' Mr Forsyth told us sternly, 'is and always has been a rutting and fighting animal,' and his manner clearly suggested that this is not only the way it is but the way he would wish it to be.

I do not know whether the programme provided anything of interest or entertainment to the listeners: the only other comment I recall was made by Miss Bakewell who, speaking about the poetry of the First World War, referred to Rupert Brooke's fighting and dying in the trenches, a piece of misinformation gleaned, I suspect, from the film version of *Oh, What a Lovely War,* which showed a mud-splattered, lugubrious Tommy reading his latest poem to his respectful mates in No-man's land: the poem was Brooke's 'The Soldier'.

When I arrived back in Berinsfield I found that the postman had delivered a considerable quantity of mail, all of it from aspiring poets and most of the envelopes containing specimens of the authors' work. Two of the letters, which did not enclose literary manuscripts, asked me to arrange suitable dates and times when their authors could visit me and bring along samples of work for my scrutiny and assessment. I began to realize that dealing with correspondence was going to take up a lot of my time.

I visited the Poetry Society at Reading University and met there for the first time in years an old friend, Ian Fletcher, and later in the week I made a new and very agreeable acquaintance at Radley School, Peter Way, the Head of the English Department there. These and the other poetry-readings and discussions I took part in seemed to be quite successful but, so far, no one in Berinsfield itself had shown any wish to solicit my services. When I was not travelling to and from the places where I was booked to appear I was kept busy reading the inexorably growing stack of manuscript poems that was being fed daily by the postman at a rate which threatened to cause me nightmares.

The quality of the work that was sent me naturally varied. A great amount of it, by young writers, was almost impossible to judge: I simply could not say whether the authors possessed any talent or not. One of the reasons for this was that the 'poems' were utterly formless. They conformed to no prescribed metrical order nor was there any discernable organization from within. In the cases where the language was stale and perfunctory it was easy enough to decide that the 'poem' was a failure, but there were examples in which the words had been chosen with some care but here the arbitrariness of the lines, their lack of either quantitative or qualitative measure, allied to a sloppiness of syntax and punctuation, usually left me baffled.

Then there were poems – most often, though not always, from older people – written in regular metres, usually with exact rhymes, employing a vocabulary and syntax that might have been unexceptional a hundred and fifty years ago but, in the nineteen-seventies, were as dusty and lifeless as dead flowers pressed between the pages of a Victorian album. Most of these works were either celebrations of natural beauty and the generosity of the Good Lord in providing such delights for mortal delectation, or warnings to the unwary against being deceived by the snares of material gain or the specious attractions of sensual indulgence and exhortations to pursue spiritual rewards. The poems tended to be rich in abstractions like *soul, beauty, truth, eternity* and so on. Some were more competently executed than others, though none was of any value except, perhaps, to its author who might have derived some pleasure or comfort from its composition.

There were a few heavily imitative pieces of writing. One young man sent me some lines which were, quite literally, poems by Dylan Thomas with a few words altered here and there, and there were quite a few clumsy imitations of Ted Hughes's *Crow* poems. In my first week's mail I found that only one of my correspondents seemed to possess any real talent and originality and it was noticeable that it was this one who appeared to be sincerely in search of practical criticism. The others, it soon became obvious, were hungry for approbation and, without exception, information on how to get their writings into print.

The desire to see his writings in print is as natural in an author as a painter's need to exhibit his work in public or a composer's to have his music performed before an audience, and the reasons for craving publication are in each case essentially the same. First, the fact that someone is prepared to risk reputation and money in presenting his work publicly is a fortifying act of faith which buttresses his confidence as an artist. Then there is the complex matter of communication. The artist, in the act of creating, in the struggle to impose order on the formlessness of the experience he wishes to explore and articulate, may not be consciously attempting to address any specific auditor or spectator; but, when the work is completed, his first impulse is to show it to someone to whom it will give delight and illumination or, perhaps, whom it will shake with pity and terror; in other words the desire to communicate, which has probably been latent during the processes of creation, now asserts itself and, with it, the simple human need for approval, admiration, and applause. These appetites – the hunger to express and then share the deepest emotional responses to experience with others, or more simply to hand on something of the pleasure that some occasion has given the artist, or even, at a less noble level, the desire to dazzle, arouse, show off – these exist, I am sure, to some degree in most artists, but they are subordinate to the primary impulse to create which is pure, self-sufficient, its own reward or punishment.

The popular legend of the starving artist in his wretched garret, whose genius is recognized only after his death, is one to which history gives little support, and there have been few such examples in the past two centuries. On the other hand, in literature, much that should never have been dignified by print has found, and still does find, acceptance. That considerable quantities of writing in both verse and prose that are quite undeserving of publication do find their way into print, either in magazines or between hard covers, must be a cause of bitter disappointment and frustration to the thousands of unpublished authors who believe, perhaps with reason, that their own work is superior to so much of what they see published. Yet I believe that the man or woman who has something that he or she feels compelled to say and has found a way of saying it freshly and memorably will, sooner or later, see the work in print if it is persistently offered to editors, and I believe that a period of rejection and neglect can be valuable as a test of seriousness and, furthermore, it might rescue the young apprentice writer from a premature public display of abortive efforts which he would later regret having exposed to general scrutiny.

The cumulative effect of reading the letters and manuscripts was one of profound depression. I felt sympathy for all of my correspondents but underneath that sympathy moved a gradually strengthening current of irritation, an irrational resentment that I should be the one who had to offer advice, encouragement or tactfully-phrased consolation. Two of the letters told me that their authors had been sending poems to magazines and publishers over a long period and their work had been consistently and unhelpfully rejected. Each of them asked the same question: should they continue writing or give up? The query, it seemed to me, provided its own answer, yet I knew that this was not what either wished to be told. I sat at my typewriter and grimly tapped out my messages of mainly false comfort and unwanted counsel. By nine o'clock I felt that I had earned a drink.

Jack Norris and Brendan Corrigan were in the Community Centre bar and we enjoyed a few convivial jars together before the club closed at ten-thirty. Then Jack suggested that Brendan and I went to his flat where we could all partake of a bottle of whisky which he had won earlier that week in a raffle. The visit would also give me an opportunity to look at his collection of first-editions and pick up the manuscript of his book on the Fair Rosamond.

Jack, who was an enthusiastic collector rather than a reader of books, owned a few interesting works, some of them quite rare, though the only one that I really coveted was a first edition of Joyce's *Ulysses*. Brendan was amiably dismissive of his friend's bookishness and he was clearly happier when we sat down to drink the whisky and talk more generally about local people and affairs and, before very long, about boxing. He had drunk a lot of Guinness at the club and the generous measures of whisky that Jack kept pouring for us began to have their effect. Gradually he became less companionable and I thought I detected a glint of belligerence in his reddening eyes. I was not deceived.

Suddenly he leaned forward in his chair and fixed me with a challenging stare. 'You,' he said, 'you was never a pro. You can't tell me you was ever a pro. Who was your manager?'

I had not had as much to drink as Brendan and felt genially relaxed. I said, 'No, I wasn't a proper pro. I didn't have more than half-a-dozen fights. I was an amateur really.'

Brendan did not look mollified. 'If you had half-a-dozen pro fights – if you had *one* pro fight – you must have had a manager!'

'He was called Wally Dakin. Used to manage a middleweight just before the war. Frank Hough. Remember him?'

If either name meant anything to Brendan he showed no sign of recognition. He said with deliberation, 'You was never a pro and you was never an amateur neither. I can tell by the look of you. Come on. Stand up. Just shape up so's I can take a look at the style of you.'

I said, 'Some other time.'

He heaved himself to his feet and placed his glass carefully on the mantelpiece. 'Just want to see the way you put your fists up, that's all. I won't hurt you. Just spar up. Come on. No need to be scared.'

Jack said, 'Forget it, Brendan. Drink your scotch. Sit down and enjoy your drink.'

'Now wait a minute. The man says he's a fighter, says he's been a pro. Well, I say he's never had the gloves on in his life. I'm not after fighting the man. I just want to take a look at the style of him. I can tell a fighter, just the way he stands.'

I said, 'Sit down. I don't care whether you think I've been in the ring. It's not me making any claims. It's what you've heard or read in the local paper. They like to make a thing about it. They think it's good publicity, the mixture; poet and pug. Frankly I'm sick of it. Whatever I was a quarter of a century ago isn't of any importance to anybody. So let's forget it and talk about something else.'

But Brendan was not to be distracted. 'Was you or was you not a pro?' he said.

'I've told you. I had a few pro fights. I held a Board of Control licence, so yes, I was a professional boxer. Briefly.'

'All right then,' Brendan exclaimed with an expression of obscure triumph, 'then stand up and show us your stance.'

'Drink up,' Jack said. 'Sit down and drink up.'

Then I had an idea. 'Look,' I said, 'when's the next training-session at the gym? I'll come along if I'm free that night and we can put the gloves on for a round. It'll have to be a short round because I'm an old man but I think I could last a minute or so. That suit you?'

Brendan was probably four or five years younger than me but he did not look in much better shape.

'Eight-ounce gloves,' he pronounced.

'I think we might be better with training-gloves.'

'Eight-ounce.'

'All right. I don't mind.'

'What about Thursday? You doing anything on Thursday night?'

'No,' I said without the least idea whether I had an engagement then or not. 'Thursday'll do fine.'

Brendan gave me a hard stare, picked up his drink and sat down, but the atmosphere was still simmering with mistrust and bellicosity so I finished my whisky, thanked Jack for his hospitality and left. It was not until I got back to the flat that I remembered that I had not collected the manuscript of *The Fair Rosamond*.

I did not meet Brendan for The Fight of the Century on the following Thursday; in fact I saw neither him nor Jack for almost a week during which I was busy giving more readings and visiting London again to record a talk on poetry for the BBC. I had done what I could to improve the flat and had telephoned Christopher Kerr of the Southern Arts Association to complain bitterly of its primitive furnishings. A couple of days later he produced carpets, lampshades and another chair. I had fixed curtains at both the bedroom and living-room windows so the place, while still far from luxurious, was beginning to look a little less unwelcoming.

I had made a few more acquaintances in Berinsfield. Two young married women had called and asked me if I would read their short stories. They both had young children and absentee husbands and both were attending part-time courses at the Oxford Polytechnic studying for O-Levels in a commendable attempt to repair the deficiencies of their earlier education. They were both pleasant girls and one of them wrote with some vigour and facility but neither had reached a stage of development in self-expression much beyond that of a moderately bright fifteen-year-old at a good school and both were handicapped by lack of the right kind of reading. There was not a lot I could do to help beyond encouraging them to continue with their efforts to write and suggesting a few authors from whose work they might possibly derive pleasure and instruction; but I sensed that they were disappointed and that they had expected from me something else, something that their teachers could not give them but I, as a man who had actually written and published books, would be able to. I told them that I would be pleased to see any of their future work and they thanked me politely and left.

My nearest neighbour, who occupied the only other flat on the ground floor, was a widow, a Mrs Fitzgerald, who was a keen churchwoman but quite untouched by the narrow puritanism that one might have expected to find in a lady of her generation and circumstances of threatened gentility. She was voluble and jolly and, on our first meeting, she asked me how I was managing domestically, especially about cooking. I told her that I was not doing too badly but that I was hampered by shortage of kitchen utensils which I hoped to acquire when I could find time to go on a shopping expedition to Oxford or Wallingford.

'What do you need?' she said. 'For goodness' sake don't go wasting your money on pots and pans because I've got some old ones I was going to throw out or give to the next jumble-sale.

You're welcome to them.' And she supplied me with a saucepan, a frying-pan and some cutlery. She also introduced me to another tenant from one of the flats in the block, a quiet middle-aged man named Tony who worked as a patrolman for the Automobile Association, and I subsequently met him and his wife quite frequently for a drink in The Berinsfield Arms. He was an ex-regular soldier and had served with the Eighth Army in the Middle East and he enjoyed recalling those eventful days with a fond nostalgia that he mistakenly believed me to share.

My casual relationship with Tony and the three or four other regular customers of the pub with whom I became reasonably friendly was secured once it was understood that I was not intent on proselytizing for poetry or the fine arts and that I could share their interest in the usual topics of bar conversation, local and national gossip, sport, the cost of living and television programmes and performers. When they grew more used to my company there would be an occasional, slightly awkward joke made about poets or poetry and, if there were no women present, a dirty story might be related and its introduction would usually contain a half-mocking, half-apologetic nod towards my innocence or spiritual nature as a poet and again I experienced that disconcerting feeling of wearing clerical garb in the pagan ambience of the pub.

Apart from the single interview with the two mature O-Level students I had not, as resident poet in Berinsfield, contributed anything at all to the community and, although there had been no more direct criticisms of my occupying a council flat – at least, none had reached my ears – I felt that my presence there might well be resented by many of the inhabitants of the village. I tried to alleviate my sense of guilt by telling myself that it was no secret that I was living in the place and that I was available to anyone, individually or collectively, who wished to make use of my presence in whatever way they desired, but the uneasy sense of being a parasite remained. So I felt some relief when, as I was entering my flat one morning after doing a little shopping at the Co-op, Mrs Fitzgerald appeared at her doorway and indicated that she would like a word with me.

'Oh Mr Scallon' – the pronunciation of my name was something she never succeeded in mastering – 'I was hoping to catch you. You know I belong – well, I don't suppose you do know – but I belong to the Ladies' Circle here and I was talking to the Secretary the other day and we wondered if you would be good enough to come and give us a talk. We usually have a speaker at our meetings. Some very good ones, too. Mrs Hodges gave us a lovely talk about her holiday in Greece last month. Colour slides and all. We did enjoy that.'

I said that I would gladly speak to the Ladies' Circle.

'Oh, that's good.' She smiled happily. 'And what would you talk to us about?'

The question surprised me. 'Well, poetry, I suppose.'

Mrs Fitzgerald's smile was instantly erased. She seemed slightly to recoil and looked almost offended as if I had made an improper suggestion. 'I don't think they'd like *that!*' she declared.

I was not at all sure how to respond to her evident horror. The only non-literary topic which I thought I could speak on with any background of knowledge and experience was pugilism and I doubted if that would be any more attractive than poetry to the Berinsfield Ladies' Circle.

I said, 'Perhaps your Secretary could telephone me some time. I expect we could arrange something.'

She nodded doubtfully and we parted. I was not surprised to hear nothing more of my addressing the Ladies' Circle.

When I next visited the Community Centre bar I wondered if Brendan would be as aggressive as when I had last seen him and if he would interpret my longish absence from the Club and my failure to show up at the gymnasium on the previous Thursday night as evidence of fear at having my spurious claim to having been a boxer put to the test. It was about nine o'clock on a Wednesday evening and the bar was quite busy. Jack Norris was there and he greeted me affably and asked me what I wanted to drink.

When I had been served I said, 'Brendan not been in tonight?'

'Not yet. He'll probably be in later. Haven't seen you for some time. Been busy?'

'I've been travelling around quite a bit and I've had a lot of mail to deal with. By the way, I forgot to take your *Fair Rosamond* away with me last time I saw you.'

'Oh, there's no hurry about it. You can pick it up some other time.'

At about half-past-nine Brendan joined us at the bar. He

spoke to me, if not effusively, with unstrained civility and we drank and chatted until closing-time.

Then Brendan suggested that we all went to his house for a drink. The invitation was offered with geniality and both Jack and I accepted. When we arrived I was introduced to Brendan's wife, Rose, and his son, the young boxer, Mel. Mrs Corrigan cut sandwiches and we sat drinking Guinness and talking desultorily until Mel yawned and said the he had better get to bed if he was going to be up in time for work next morning. It was after his departure that Brendan's manner changed, not immediately or dramatically, but I suddenly noticed that he was watching me with a kind of calculating intentness and that the timbre of his voice had very slightly changed, had become harder, an instrument for probing rather than communicating.

He began to speak of technicalities of the fight game, the treatment of facial cuts, methods of training, the permitted length of bandages for the hands and how best to apply them, and it soon became obvious to me that his intention was not to make conversation but to uncover my ignorance of these matters.

Jack's attempts to divert the discourse into more pacific areas were trampled under the weight of Brendan's determination to reach his goal of once again challenging me to prove myself and, before long, he was repeating his suspicion, or rather his certainty, that I had never been in a boxing-ring in my life. By this time I had drunk enough to awaken an answering, though modified, pugnacity. It was a curious feeling of affable, almost jocular aggression. I felt both annoyed by, yet even more friendly towards Brendan. He was a good man. But his accusing looks were becoming irritating. And comical. His earnestness, the bellicose suspicion, the apparent sense of insult and indignation seemed funnier and funnier. I think it was my visible amusement that sparked off the action.

I cannot remember how we reached the point of standing and facing each other with fists at the ready but we did.

Rose was saying, 'Oh my God! Brendan! Will you stop it now! Brendan! You hear me! There's to be no fighting here!'

Brendan ignored his wife. 'I can tell by the looks of you,' he said to me, 'the way you stand, the way you hold your mitts. Never had 'em on in your life!'

He flicked a contemptuous left lead at me. I deflected it and

35

countered, very lightly with the open left hand. And that started it. Brendan was not the man to fool around with playful, open-handed sparring. He came forward with fists bunched into knuckled weapons, prodding out a measuring left and getting ready to throw a big right hand that would switch all my lights out for a minute or so. Again I deflected the left lead and jabbed his head back with my own left and, instinctively, found myself hooking off the jab with the same fist. The hook made him stagger sideways. I caught a glimpse of his face, scarlet with rage, eyes bulging with vengeful resolve, and he came at me swinging wildly with both fists. I took a couple of paces back, keeping outside the swings, then stepped inside with a short right to the chin and Brendan was on the floor and Rose was screaming, 'Mel! Mel!' and I was saying to myself, 'Jesus! What have I done now!'

The living-room door flew open and Mel charged in as his father was heaving himself laboriously to his feet. The boy's eyes were sparking with fury as he swung towards me.

'No, Mel!' Rose shouted. 'No! It was your father's fault! He asked for it! It was his own fault! He started it!'

I felt Jack's hand on my sleeve. 'Come on,' he muttered, 'let's get out of here.'

By this time Brendan was up and mouthing threats and imprecations.

'Yes, please go,' Rose was imploring. 'You'd better go. I'm sorry. Please go now.'

Jack and I left the house.

I felt the atavistic excitement draining rapidly away. The night air was shiveringly cold.

I said, 'That was a mistake. I should never have gone back there. I should have known.'

'Don't worry. Brendan'll be okay. He'll probably have forgotten all about it tomorrow.'

I was not convinced.

We said goodnight and I went back to the flat. I was feeling depressed and self-disgusted by then. What the hell was I was doing in Berinsfield anyway? I didn't belong there. I hadn't been in a brawl for years and it was inexcusable to get into one at my age. It was demeaning, brutish, stupid. I ought to be able to handle a situation like the one with Brendan without swapping punches like a Friday-night navvy. And it had happened just as I was beginning to think that Berinsfield might be a tolerable place to live and work in for a few months. I had balls-ed everything up by making an enemy. It was no use offering the excuse that Brendan had been the instigator. I didn't blame him for doubting my credentials as a boxer. It was natural that he should see only an effetely arty man, a poet, bookworm, probably a pouf. You didn't see people of that kind around the gyms, the boxing-clubs and arenas.

I undressed and went to bed. I would apologize to Brendan the next time I saw him. Or should I try to avoid seeing him? Impossible in a place as small as Berinsfield. Maybe I could let him have a smack at me, a kind of penalty-punch. What a fool I'd been. But I was tired and I had a lot of work to do the next day, more manuscripts to read, letters to write and a visit to the Wallingford Arts Club in the evening.

Then, just as I was sinking into sleep, I was suddenly snatch-ed back into wakefulness and I was startled by a brief, small but unmistakable glow of elation, and I found myself thinking: 'Well, well, I might be a beat-up old sod but I can still move a bit when it comes to the push!' and I knew that I was grinning triumphantly in the darkness. But, before I could chastise myself for such reprehensible sentiments, I was asleep.

The next day one of the producers of the BBC radio programme, 'Kaleidoscope', telephoned to say that on the following Sunday evening Paul Scofield would be reading, on Radio 3, Gerard Manley Hopkins's poem, 'The Wreck of the Deutschland', and, on the next morning, there was to be a memorial tablet to the great Jesuit poet unveiled in West-minster Abbey. Would I listen to the broadcast of the poem and also attend the ceremony at the Abbey and talk about both events on Monday evening's programme. I agreed and, on Sun-day, December 7th, settled down to listen to the actor reading Hopkins's poem dedicated

To the
happy memory of five Franciscan nuns
exiled by the Falck Laws
drowned between midnight and morning of
Dec. 7th, 1875.

I confess that I felt some trepidation. Generally I prefer to read poetry for myself and do not care to hear it spoken aloud, unless it is dramatic verse specifically intended for declamation, but all of my prejudices were obliterated by Scofield's lucid, restrained and intelligent speaking of the lines which present to any reader formidable difficulties with their variety and subtleties of rhythm and odd syntactical constructions.

The next morning I had to rise early and drive to London. I parked in the car park at Paddington Station and took a taxi to the Abbey where a seat had been reserved for me quite close to the pulpit from which the service was to be conducted. It was a truly ecumenical occasion with as many Roman Catholic clergy as Anglican present. The service began with the hymn, 'Praise to the Holiest in the Height', the words of which had been composed by another famous convert, Cardinal Newman; then, after the Welcome by the Dean of Westminster and a reading from *Ecclesiasticus* 44: v. 1-15, beginning with the familiar: 'Let us now praise famous men...',Sir John Gielgud read some Hopkins, including 'Heaven-Haven', 'God's Grandeur' and 'The Windhover'. After that a procession of dignitaries moved to Poets' Corner where the Memorial was unveiled by the Duke of Norfolk. The ceremony completed, Peter Levi, the poet and Jesuit priest, delivered the Address after which Gielgud read more Hopkins, quite well but not, I thought, with the insight, eloquence and clarity that Scofield had displayed in his broadcast. The service ended with prayers and the Blessing.

I went straight from the Abbey to Broadcasting House to record my piece for that evening and I was out of the studio in time to have a drink in The George before it closed at 3 pm. As usual the bar was quite full but I saw no one there whom I knew and I thought it was just as well since I did not want to be tempted by some old boozing-partner to extend my London visit by embarking on a large-scale bender. But I was aware, too, of a feeling of mild disappointment. Things were not as once they had been and that, too, was probably just as well. And yet regret persisted. I looked with disfavour at the young 'executives' in their snappy suits and fashionable hair-styles and moustaches, sipping their well-advertised drinks and smoking their well-advertised small cigars, and I mourned for

38

the old scruffy George and the old drinking-companions, so
many of them now dead: Louis MacNeice, most reticent and
ironic of grey eminences, whose cagey leashing of words and
feelings might have fooled those who did not know him that he
was a cold man; John Davenport, in exile from a previous, more
rumbustious age, carrying with him the weight of the failure of
his youthful promise with dignity and good humour, totally
without self-pity and generously discerning of other people's
talent, of Burns Singer's for instance, another George habitué,
now with the long sleepers, the promise of whose poetry has yet
to be recognized by more than a very few; W. R. Rodgers,
known to his friends by the improbable, music-hall name of
Bertie, unlikely former pastor, gifted poet and quiet wit; Julian
Maclaren-Ross, the one-man cast of a continuous private
movie, skilled with the pen but stupefying with the tongue; and
many other affable familiar ghosts including, of course, the
presiding spirit, the little Welsh Falstaff, Dylan Thomas. For a
moment I was tempted to go to the ML Club in the vain hope of
resurrecting something of the past but common sense interven-
ed and I recalled that the ML had changed even more than The
George, so I left the pub and took an underground train to Pad-
dington where I picked up the van and drove back to
Berinsfield.

During the drive I found myself thinking of the unveiling
ceremony for Gerard Manley Hopkins and then of that other,
secular shrine of departed poets, The George, in which the
Jesuit priest would have felt as out of place as a ballerina in a
rugby-scrum. It was treacherously easy in middle-age to fall
into the trap of sentimentally mythologizing those raffish
ghosts of the literary underworld, to forget that one was engag-
ed in an editing of the past, a rewriting of one's youth, so that
the story appeared more eventful, colourful and heroic than it
had really been. This is not to say, of course, that none of those
Bohemian roaring-boys possessed singularity of character and
real talent; most of them did, a few abundantly, but the roman-
tic backward look was selective and myopic so that the
blemishes were either invisible or changed, the pustule become
a beauty-spot. The *poète maudit*, the tormented, self-destructive
bard, is not a romantic invention but among poets of stature,
outside fiction, he is to be found in far fewer numbers than the
hard-working, abstemious, responsible man and, while he may

be splendid company in the pages of literary biography, he could often be a sore trial to those who knew him in the probably malodorous flesh.

The truth is, surely, that it is better to know authors from a long and deep association with their writings, in which is distilled the best of what they have thought and felt, the best of what they are, than from personal knowledge. I thank Providence that I was never in the company of Evelyn Waugh, though I owe him a vast debt of gratitude for the pleasure he has given me, through his work. However, it is a marvellous experience to make the personal acquaintance of a writer whose work you have long admired and to find him, not only likable and admirable, but prepared to give generously of his friendship, and I shall be forever thankful that this happened to me when, early in 1966, I met Edmund Blunden for the first time.

The Arts Council had invited me to accompany Blunden on a poetry-reading tour of the North-West and Midlands and I was both delighted and apprehensive at the prospect of travelling with and appearing on the same platform as a poet who belonged to the heroic generation of the First Word War, a figure who seemed to me almost as remote and mythical as the great and tragic revenants of No-man's Land, Wilfred Owen, Edward Thomas and Isaac Rosenberg. I remembered vividly my first reading of Blunden's prose masterpiece, *Undertones of War*, at a time when the allied struggle against Hitler had just begun in that long, mockingly beautiful summer of 1940, at the end of which I was myself to become a soldier at the age of eighteen, the same age that Blunden had been in 1914. I had found in his poetry much to admire and enjoy though I could see that it possessed some features that would perhaps cause many readers, whose tastes had been conditioned by post-imagist verses, to undervalue it; indeed, before I could properly enter Blunden's poetic world I had to re-attune my ear so that it would not be disconcerted by occasionally archaic phrasing and rhythmic echoes of the eighteenth century, but once this adjustment had been made the rewards were substantial, a music, freshness of vision, a sense of wisdom and innocence that had been almost entirely missing from English poetry for a century and a half, and an unobtrusive but highly developed formal skill that few of his more highly regarded contemporaries could begin to rival.

But it was about the man rather than his work that I was thinking as I drove along the M40 motorway. I remembered our meeting in the Piccadilly Hotel in Manchester at the beginning of the tour. Edmund had travelled by train from his home in Long Melford in Sussex and I had driven from Surrey but, from then onwards, we were to journey together in my car. I knew, from what I had read of him, that he was not physically a large man, but he was smaller, more stooped and older than I had expected. But any impression of decrepitude that I might have gained from his frailty and white hair was at once and permanently obliterated by his shrewd, good-humoured vitality, by his lively curiosity about everything and everyone around him, the zest with which he spoke on all manner of topics and with which he looked forward to our expedition.

It soon transpired that Edmund was an enthusiastic beer drinker and, on that first night, after we had given our reading, we returned to the hotel and sat drinking bitter until well past midnight. This was to set the pattern of many more convivial sessions when we chatted easily about literature, love, life and, of course, war. The Great War was, understandably enough, the one huge dominating event of his life: it overshadowed, permeated, haunted, judged and accused all that had occurred since. It soon became clear that Edmund Blunden, poet and scholar, most congenial of drinking-companions, keen cricketer, loving husband and father was, above all, a man in deep and ceaseless mourning for the countless dead of World War One. Not that he in any way dramatized his grief or his own experiences. In fact he spoke scarcely at all of his own participation in the war, only in general terms of the waste, futility and horror, and of the courage, dignity and strength that flowered incredibly in that abominable wilderness. I was acutely aware of the paucity of my own battle experience compared with the nightmare of suffering, terror and privation that he, as a very young man, had endured, yet never, for an instant, did he make me feel less than his equal.

It was the same when we spoke of poetry. We found – and his delight seemed as great as mine at the discovery – that we shared a love of many English poets though each of us had reservations, in some cases quite strong ones, about an idol of the other's. At no time did he by word or expression hint that his opinion might be weightier than mine. I never heard him, nor could I imagine him, express any judgement that contained the slightest element of malice. He was the most modest, courteous, and generous man I have ever met or will be likely to meet and it was impossible not to love him.

The last time I saw Edmund was in the summer of 1971. I had been in Norfolk acting as a tutor with Alan Brownjohn and Ted Walker on a poetry course; Ted was giving me a lift in his car to London when I realized that Long Melford was not very much out of our way. I suggested to Ted that we call on Blunden, whom I had not seen for some time, and he readily agreed.

The old poet had been appointed to the Chair of Poetry at Oxford in 1966 but ill-health had forced him to relinquish it after a couple of years and I heard that he was far from well. I therefore thought it prudent to telephone from Long Melford and find out from Edmund's wife, Claire, whether or not a visit would be welcome. She assured me at once that I need have no doubts on that score so Ted and I bought some beer from an off-licence and, a few moments later, we were knocking on the door of Hall Mill, the Blundens' home.

Edmund had changed since I had last seen him but he had not essentially altered: he had become intensified. His white hair, always profuse, was whiter and more abundant, his eyes not faded, as the eyes of the aged so often fade, but brighter than I remembered them, and his nose, never his least prominent feature, was now vast, aquiline, commanding. The set of his head was proud and defiant, it spoke of energy in repose. He looked very old, older than his temporal age of seventy-five, but he was unconquered and unconquerable. He looked tired and battered, perhaps tormented by the years, but he was still very much alive, still ready to 'spit into the face of Time', like Yeats's Old Pensioner. For many years he had suffered from severe bronchial trouble and now his voice had sunk to the faintest hoarse whisper, a ghost of a voice. It was not easy to communicate but I do not think that this worried any of us. We sat for half-an-hour or so and drank our beer; Ted or Claire or I did most of the talking and Edmund listened and smiled and occasionally commented in that strained, spectral voice that was often inaudible to me but, through the telepathy of love and long familiarity, audible and comprehensible to his wife. Then, as Ted and I were preparing to leave, Edmund indicated that he wished to show something to Ted.

He led us into the room where he kept some of the treasures of his John Clare collection. He pointed with pride to a fine painting in oils of the poet and then to another picture, this one of an owl, that had been given to him by Clare's grandson. The head of the owl, full-face, was superbly done, the eyes haunting and strangely mesmeric. I had seen both paintings on my first visit to Hall Mill but I found the bird no less powerful, balefully beautiful, and I knew that Ted was just as impressed. We stood there for some time, fixed by the owl's stare. Then, as we turned away, Edmund said, in his faint, crepitant whisper, but quite distinctly, 'He's a good old owl.'

When we left, Claire and Edmund walked with us to the garden gate. Progress was slow; the old poet required the support of his wife's hand and his footsteps were uncertain. We exchanged farewells and Ted and I moved away to where we had left our car. Before I climbed in I looked back and waved. Edmund raised his hand in answering salute, the small figure with the noble white head, frail but indomitable. I got into the car and we drove away.

We were silent for a few moments. Then Ted spoke. 'He's a good old owl,' he said.

That evening I went to the Club. When I arrived I saw that Brendan was standing at the bar with his customary Guinness. I felt a flicker of guilty apprehension. I could not blame him if he were feeling more than a little resentful after our last engagement. But there was no sign of hostility in his grin when he saw me hesitating in the entrance and waved me over.

'What you drinking?' he asked.

I said that I would have a pint of bitter. 'I've been to London,' I told him. I wanted to suggest that I had been away from Berinsfield for a few days and had not been deliberately avoiding him.

'Oh yes. Jack was saying the other day we hadn't seen you lately. You had a good time?'

'Yes. All right. Has Jack been in tonight?'

'I haven't seen him.'

'I want to get that thing he's written. I promised him I'd have

43

a look at it.'

Brendan nodded. His manner was quite friendly, though I thought I sensed a kind of reserve. He was smiling faintly, inwardly, as if at some private joke.

I drank some bitter and then said awkwardly, 'Sorry about the other night. Too much to drink. I can't hold it the way I used to.'

He chuckled. 'I think we'd all had enough. Nothing to worry about.' He touched the side of his jaw delicately. 'That's a hell of a wallop you've got there.' There was no trace of rancour in his voice. He sounded as though he was complimenting me on something I was wearing, a new tie perhaps or a smart suit.

I said again, 'Sorry. It shouldn't have happened. I don't go in for –'

He interrupted. 'Not at all! Nothing to be sorry about. Forget it. It was my own fault anyway. Listen, you've not seen my boy, Mel, work out yet. They're training tomorrow night. Can you make it then?'

I said that I could.

'I'll see you about seven. I want him to get really fit this year for the ABA Championships. He's got a good chance. I know he's my boy but there's others as'll tell you the same. He's in with a real chance this year. I'd like you to come and see him next time he's got a contest. I'd like your opinion.' He would like my opinion, as someone who had some knowledge of the game. This was Brendan's way of apologizing for questioning my credentials.

I said, 'I'd like to see him. We must arrange something next time he's fighting.'

Presently we were joined by Jack who said that he had been watching a television play and had not noticed how late it was. We had two or three more drinks before the barman called time and we emptied our glasses and went out into the cold December night.

'See you tomorrow then,' Brendan said.

I told him I would be at the gymnasium at seven and we said goodnight and separated.

When I got back to the flat I made myself a mug of coffee and brought out the diary I had started to keep and wrote in it briefly an account of the past forty-eight hours. Then I read Gerard Manley Hopkins's *Collected Poems* until sleepiness made concentration impossible and I closed the book and went to bed.

I woke up at seven-thirty in the morning feeling quite cheerful and physically well. I drank some fresh orange juice, made a pot of tea and boiled an egg which I ate with buttered cream-crackers. I had found that I ate so little bread that, if I bought a loaf, it would be stale and inedible before I had eaten a quarter of it, so I had given up bread in favour of crackers which kept fresh for so much longer. The mail arrived, with a little rush and snap from the letter-box, and I poured myself another cup of tea which I sipped while I was tearing open the envelopes and examining their contents. There were three more invitations to give readings, two in Oxford and one at a school in Newbury, a letter with accompanying poems from a lady in Burnley and one without poems from a man in Buckinghamshire who said that he would like to visit me and bring some of his work for criticism. There was a telephone number printed at the head of his notepaper so I decided that I would ring him up later and save myself the trouble of writing. Then I remembered that I had an appointment that day at two o'clock with a lady who had written from a vicarage a few miles away and was probably the vicar's wife.

I read the Burnley lady's poems which I found very touching in an innocent and unfashionable way and I wrote to say that I had enjoyed her work but was doubtful of its chances of publication with any of the larger commercial firms. I enclosed the addresses of a few magazines that I thought might be interested in her poems and also details of the few small presses I knew about who were quite honest and not out to trap and exploit the unwary amateur. By one o'clock I had dealt with all unanswered mail and, with the satisfying feeling of having completed a tedious chore, I left the flat, crossed the road to the pillar-box into which I dropped my morning's work, and then went on to the The Berinsfield Arms for a pint of beer and some bread and cheese. By two o'clock I was back in the flat waiting for my visitor and looking at the living-room in an attempt to see it through the eyes of someone entering it for the first time.

What I saw gave me no pleasure. The drabness of the wallpaper had not been much alleviated by the few reproductions I had stuck on the walls, and the untidiness of my books and papers, the brown, circular coffee stains on the table, could not, I felt compelled to admit, be seen as picturesque and bohemian disorder. It was an ill-furnished, gloomy and uncomfortable place and only ambitious and expensive redecorating and furnishing could effect a real improvement. Its only possible advantage over more attractive rooms, I reflected, was that it might discourage unwelcome callers from staying longer than the purpose of the visit strictly necessitated.

There was a knock on the door and I opened it to admit the lady from the vicarage. My first surprise was that she was younger than I had expected, and my second that she did not, in her dress and person, fulfil my expectations of what a vicar's wife would look like. She wore jeans and a sweater under an anorak that was rather grubby and creased. Jeans and sweater can be the uniform of non-conformity – if the paradox is permissible – or they can serve as provocative packaging for girls who wish to advertise their physical assets persuasively and comparatively inexpensively, but it was quite obvious that this girl wore the garments for reasons of utility and no other. The jeans were shabby and not noticeably well-fitting and the shapeless hairy sweater could have accommodated another person of the same size. She looked to be in her middle twenties and she had short unkempt hair, a pleasant, snub-nosed urchin's face, and she showed none of the self-consciousness that might forgivably have been displayed by a young woman who had come to solicit the literary advice and criticism of a total stranger.

Her first words were, 'May I use your lavatory?'

When she had returned from this necessary errand I made us a mug of coffee each and we seated ourselves at my working table and, after an exchange of generalities during which I discovered that she was the daughter and not the wife of the vicar, she produced her poems. I was relieved to see that there were not many and that they were all fairly short; I was even more relieved when I discovered, as I read through them, that they were decidedly interesting, that she cared about language and she was concerned with subjects outside the dark and narrow area of her own emotional states. It was good to be able to tell her with sincerity that I liked her work. I made one or two suggestions about possible rephrasing – probably the only useful kind of criticism that anyone can offer – and I gave her the addresses of some magazines to which she might submit her poems for consideration. Then we talked a little about her reading and I was able to recommend a few writers from whom she might gain pleasure and profit. She was serious without being over-earnest, intelligent and unaffected, and after she had left I felt that perhaps there might be some point in my being available to people like her, young women and men who were resolved to write seriously but whose circumstances isolate them from anyone with similar interests with whom they could exchange ideas and encouragement.

At seven o'clock I walked along to the Community Centre gymnasium. Before I entered the building I could hear distantly those echoing sounds that could still set my pulses racing and touch my palate with the taste of excitement, the irregular rhythms of padded fists thumping the heavy bag, the fast, steady tempo of speedball and skipping rope, its swish and slap counterpointed against the tattoo of the dancing feet, the gruff exhortations of the trainer. It was a harsh music whose echoes I could faintly hear, sounds from childhood and young manhood that would never fail to touch my imagination, stirring again those ancient hopes and fears, bringing back the flavours of apprehension, exultation, triumph and defeat. And it was not only the ring-adventures that were revivified: the whole of childhood and adolescence could somehow be unlocked by those sounds and the images they engendered, the mystery, the terror, the piercing sweetness, the bewilderment, the blind yearnings because, from puberty onwards, all of experience – imaginative, physical, erotic – all were enacted against the omnipresence of the Game which seemed to embrace or symbolize all human activity, sensation and aspiration.

But when I got inside the gym I was disappointed. The club where I had trained as a boy and young man had been a ramshackle old building in Aylesbury. There had been no proper dressing-rooms, no showers, and the rings – there had been two, one for juniors and one for seniors – had been erected at ground level and each was enclosed by a single, unpadded rope which could cause painful 'burns' on your back if you allowed yourself to be forced against it. The heavy punch-bag had been improvised from an old army kit-bag and the sparring gloves were ancient, uncomfortable to wear and a lot more uncomfortable to be hit by, but the place had always been vibrant with active enthusiasm. It had been a serious business: trainers,

47

boxers, committee members, all of them had been there because it was important to them that they should be, for some of them perhaps the most important thing in their lives. The Berinsfield boxing club was different.

The gymnasium was large with a high ceiling. Badminton courts had been marked out on the floor and there was plenty of equipment for all kinds of physical activity: climbing-ropes, vaulting-horses and boxes, wall-bars, horizontal and so on. The boxing club used only a small part of the gymnasium and, in this section, there were three punch-bags of varying weights, but no boxing-ring of any kind. The boys who had turned up for the training-session were, with the exception of Mel Corrigan, who was about twenty, all very young, their ages ranging between about ten and sixteen, and few of them seemed to be taking matters with any seriousness. The man whose voice I had heard shouting commands was not the official trainer but the father of one of the youngest boys and he was doing his best to impose some method on the evening's activities, but with only limited success. Brendan was timing his son who was punching the heaviest of the bags. When the boy had finished this part of his programme he skipped for three three-minute rounds, subjected himself to a series of torturing abdominal exercises on the floor and then went away to get changed. I had noticed that he worked with a dogged intensity, permitting himself no respite, but there had been a kind of resentment about his efforts, a sense of reluctance overcome with difficulty. No fighter can be said to enjoy training: the process is too painful for enjoyment. Yet he must work with a kind of zest which at times of extremity can become something very close to a self-flagellant ecstasy.

Brendan said, 'The bloody trainer's not turned up again. It's a terrible thing. How do you expect the kids to train if your man's not there himself? What kind of an example's that at all?'

I thought it might be politic to change the subject. 'Mel looked in pretty good shape.'

'And that's another thing. Nobody to spar with him. The other seniors have packed it in. And who could be blaming the lads? How can the kid train when he can't get sparring? What's the use in that? It makes you bloody sick.'

We left the gym and went to the Club bar. I felt some relief when Jack came in and Brendan was distracted from his monotonous tirade against the criminal irresponsiblity of the boxing trainer and began to mellow under the influence of Guinness. A few of the other Club members included me in their greetings of Jack and Brendan as they came to the bar to order their drinks and I thought that, at last, I was beginning to be accepted as a member of the community, though there was not the least sign that anyone wished to confer with me in my role as Poet-in-Residence.

In the last two weeks before I went home for the Christmas holiday I felt that acceptance was becoming more general and unqualified in the village and, while I still found Berinsfield and the flat depressing to live in, there were aspects of both that were slowly beginning to exercise an ambiguous attraction. For the first time since my days in the army I was spending most of my leisure-time in an exclusively masculine ambience that was, for the most part, culturally and intellectually primitive. These unaccustomed circumstances began to arouse curious feelings of nostalgia and I found myself with increasing frequency thinking of my childhood and youth, the greater part of which had been spent in a not dissimilar atmosphere of cultural twilight. There still existed, I was surprised to discover, a part of me that was drawn to the thoughtless, profane and sentimental company of men to whom all art was a mystery as incomprehensible as the arcana of advanced science or philosophy, whose dichromatic moral world was of breathtaking simplicity and brutality. Perhaps it was the childishness, the almost innocence, those manifestations of tenderness and cruelty, loyalty and altruism, wild rage and hilarity which seemed to offer a re-entry to a pre-lapsarian state that I had forgotten; or maybe it was something much simpler, a revulsion against the devious, ambiguous, sly and affected society in which the serious professional writer, unless he is very fortunate, must spend much of his time, a desire to feed, for a time, on plainer fare and to breathe what seemed to be a cleaner atmosphere.

The flat was no less bleak and yet it offered something that I had been deprived of for so long that I had almost forgotten its savour: solitude. I relished it but I could not turn it to my advantage. In retrospect it seems that I should have been able to find ample time in which to write whatever I wished to, and, in the purely chronological sense, such time was quite often

49

available. There I was, entirely on my own with a roof over my head, a chair and table, paper, pen and typewriter, no immediate financial worries, no tedious hack-work to be done; what more could any writer wish for? Well, there was something more, though what it was is not easy to define. The ugliness of my surroundings, both in and out of doors, was not a help, but that alone would not have prevented me from working. It was more to do with the kind of ugliness, its sterility, its lifelessness. I had lived in squalid conditions and unlovely surroundings before, in Leeds, for instance, and the less salubrious suburbs of London, and had not been inhibited from working. But however superficially grim the urban or suburban landscape had been, it had possessed a vital element, a vigour and sometimes even a jagged beauty which could stimulate, and it had been, to some extent, an expression of the lives of the people who occupied it. Not so with Berinsfield. That penal-looking architecture had been planned and erected without reference to the people who were to inhabit it. It had not grown but been constructed, utilitarian, complete, unchangeable, and it stifled and limited the lives of its occupants. The climate that we all breathed was infected with the slow poison of inertia. Daily I grew more lethargic.

I tried to force myself to write but, by the time I had dealt with correspondence, my energies seemed exhausted. I did manage to keep up the regular entries in my diary and I scratched away for a few hours at some protean verses, but I was increasingly aware of the spreading paralysis of the creative will and I began to wonder if I would be able to last out the nine months of my Fellowship and, if I did, what the effect on me would be. At least, I told myself, I would have a week or so of respite and regeneration at Christmas and, on my return, I would not have the same problems to face that had met me on my arrival in November. So far there had been no more overt protests about my having been given a council flat and I had, it seemed, been accepted by many of the Berinsfield people. Perhaps, after the holiday, I would be refreshed and even capable, in some way, of justifying my presence in the community.

THREE

WHEN I RETURNED TO Berinsfield the new year had begun
and with it the first cruelly cold weather of the winter. The flat
looked even more dismal than I had remembered it and the
'village' itself seemed more than ever like a prison camp. I had
served only two months of my sentence: seven more to run, and
no remission for good behaviour. Yet I knew that it was both
shameful and absurd to feel sorry for myself. I had accepted the
Fellowship gladly and, when I paused to reflect, I knew that I
was very fortunate. Although I was kept busier than I had an-
ticipated with poetry-readings, correspondence and interviews
with embryonic poets, I was not committed to regular working-
hours and the tasks I was called on to perform were not deman-
ding. Compared with wage-earners who worked in factories,
offices or on the land I led a very soft life indeed, but this
knowlege was not entirely consoling for it brought with it a dis-
turbing itch of guilt. Had I been sincerely convinced that I was
fulfilling a useful function as Resident Poet I would have felt
less uneasy, but the whole concept of such a role possessing
value was becoming in my eyes more doubtful: it sometimes
seemed to me the kind of notion that could be professed only by
those who understood little about poetry and the ways it
operated and even less about the needs of the fitters, welders,
labourers and layabouts of Berinsfield or anywhere else for that
matter.

The only occasions when my pessimistic view of the poet's
social or educative usefulness suffered revision was when I
visited schools and found – as almost invariably I did find – an
unself-conscious interest in and keen response to the poetry
that I talked about and read to my audiences, and the younger
the children the greater their enthusiasm and enjoyment. With
the older pupils, in their early teens, it was sometimes necessary
to overcome an initial resistance based largely, in the case of
boys, on the suspicion that both the production and con-
sumption of poetry were unmanly activities and could be left to
girls or sissies. In fact this attitude was much less prevalent than
when I was a schoolboy and I did not encounter much difficulty
in breaking it down in all except a few stubborn cases; the yet

older children in the upper forms had usually passed beyond this stage, if they had ever been through it, and were among the most receptive audiences I addressed. I decided that, if my stay in Berinsfield was going to serve any useful purpose, the only means of accomplishing anything would be through the young.

I telephoned the Headmaster of the Berinsfield Junior School and suggested to him that I might pay a visit and speak and read to some of his pupils. He accepted the offer promptly, a date was fixed and I conducted a most agreeable session with a group of eleven-year-olds, all of whom seemed to enjoy the occasion and, a week or two later, I was asked to return for a similar event involving some of the children who had missed my previous appearance and, apparently, had protested at being excluded. They listened attentively to what I had to say about the ways in which poetry can be made and the effects it can produce in its readers and when the time came for questions they showed no trace of shyness.

I was in the club a few days after my second visit to the school when one of the members, someone with whom I had previously had no conversation, came up to me and said, 'Hear you were up at the school the other day. George, that's my youngest, he told me you was there, Said it was great. Really enjoyed it, he did.'

A few days later I was buying some supplies in the Co-op when the young woman who was serving me said, 'I wonder if you'd come and read some poetry to our Rangers. It'd make a change for them. They've never had anything like that before.'

'To your...?'

'Rangers. You know, like the Girl Guides but a bit older. I'd be very grateful if you could come. It's a job keeping them from getting bored. Something a bit different'd be a tonic.'

An audience of teenage girls, none of whom presumably had any interest in literature, would probably be difficult to entertain, but I was pleased at being given another opportunity to do something in the community and I said that I would be glad to go along to one of their meetings. A date was arranged and again I felt unsure of what approach to adopt when I went into the Rangers' Headquarters and was seated before a semi-circle of girls who looked at me with sidelong curiosity and exchanged muttered observations and giggles as I cleared my throat and began my doubtfully focused address.

I was accustomed to audiences of children who were either genuinely interested in the stranger from a world beyond their schoolroom and home or were at least prepared to simulate attentiveness if only to placate the supervising teacher; to sixth-formers or more advanced students who possessed, to some degree, a real interest in and knowledge of literature, or to assemblies of adults who had come voluntarily and, in some cases, even paid to come and listen. The Rangers were something else. I doubted if many had read any kind of book since leaving school and I had the uncomfortable feeling that I was on display as a representative of a strange species rather than as an ordinary man who might be able to interest or divert them for half-an-hour or so. It was a long half-hour.

Speaking as simply as I could, but trying to avoid any note of patronage, I emphasized that poetry was able to give its readers a special kind of pleasure and excitement, that there were many kinds of poetry and the sort that would give enjoyment to each of the Rangers existed somewhere. It was worth looking for. I told them that I read more poetry than anything else, not because I thought it was in some way good for me, but simply because it gave me more delight than any other kind of literature. I read Hardy's 'The Oxen' to show how a poet could deal with a big subject in a very simple way. Hardy, sixty years ago, felt about religious faith as so many people in the nineteen-seventies feel: the intellect has rejected the rational bases of belief, yet the imagination and sensibility yearn for the simple faith that has almost been extinguished. Hardy uses no abstractions in the poem, no rhetoric or flamboyant imagery, yet those few lines say more about faith and its lack, about the human thirst for the ancient certainties, than whole pages of prose could hope to say.

I went on to read Ben Jonson's lines from 'A Celebration of Charis' hoping that these might at least speak to those girls who were in love:

> 'Have you seen but a bright lily grow
> Before rude hands have touched it?
> Have you marked but the fall o' snow
> Before the soil hath smutched it?
> Have you felt the wool of the beaver,
> Or swan's down ever?

> *Or have smelt o' the bud o' brier,*
> *Or the nard in the fire?*
> *Or have tasted the bag of the bee?*
> *O so white, O so soft, O so sweet is she!'*

Then I tried to show how little the heart's affections change over the centuries by giving them love poems by Robert Graves and W. H. Auden; I tried some jokey pieces by Gavin Ewart and John Betjeman and finished by reading two of my own things with an account of how they came to be written and a little about the problems of finding the right forms for them. During my commentary I tried a couple of pleasantries, both of which were received with uniform blankness. The girls were not, I felt, hostile but simply untouched, untouchable. I was sweating by the time I finished talking. No one wished to ask questions. The Ranger-Leader, or whatever her proper title should be, thanked me and I left. Two days later I saw John Wright in The Berinsfield Arms.

'I hear you gave a talk to our Rangers,' he said.

I nodded but did not say what a harrowing experience it had been for me and my audience.

'They were very disappointed it was so short, they wanted you to go on and read a lot more poems.'

'Where did you hear that?' I must have looked incredulous.

'From the girl who runs the Rangers. She said they were all too shy to ask you to go on but that's what they wanted. They complained after you'd left. Said she should have asked you to read more poems.'

'Well, I'm damned. I thought they were bored rigid.'

'Not at all. I promise you. They loved it.'

This information gave me an intensity of pleasure that surprised me and I had noticed that, after my two appearances at the school, many of the local children would greet me in the street with the greatest friendliness.

Jack and Brendan were now drinking companions and at last I managed to remember to collect the manuscript of Jack's book on the Fair Rosamond. I took it back to the flat and opened it with curiosity. It was handwritten with careful penmanship in a manner that reminded me of the handwriting of Frederick Rolfe, Baron Corvo, which I had seen in facsimile. The text was accompanied by the author's own illustrations, wood-cuts and pen-and-ink sketches, all competent and some quite handsome. The written content was not, as I suspected, of any great interest, consisting mainly of a short biography of his subject, that had been paraphrased, I guessed, from Thomas Deloney's ballad in Percy's *Reliques* and perhaps from Samuel Daniel's 'Complaynt of Roasamond' followed by a vaguely romantic account of his own obsession with the lady, all presented in a prose style which was meant to be sonorous but, influenced as it was by the nineteenth-century essayists he so much admired, emerged as strained and turgid. The book was a curiosity but not one that could conceivably interest a respectable publisher. When I told this to Jack, as gently as I could, he accepted the verdict with apparent unconcern and the work was not again referred to by either of us.

I had been back in Berinsfield for about three weeks when I was telephoned by *The Sunday Times* and asked if I would care to review the 'autobiography' of Muhammed Ali along with a book about the World Champion by Wilfred Sheed. The invitation was welcome: I was finding serious work just as difficult to tackle as I had found it before Christmas and, when I was not away from Berinsfield fulfilling engagements to give readings or talks, I was too easily tempted to spend my time in the pub or Club. So the prospect of reading the two books and writing a review of them was an agreeable one.

The 'autobiography', predictably called *The Greatest,* was ghosted by Richard Durham, a black journalist and playwright who had spent six years as a member of Ali's entourage, recording on tape and in notebook the champion's own account of his life and then setting it down in the first person as if Ali himself were the author. Not that the resulting book was a transcript of those tapes or a recital of facts: Mr Durham was out to produce literature, not mere reportage, and the style he used was one more commonly found in fiction, with plenty of direct speech and, in the description of the fights, a profusion of scattily pretentious metaphor which read like a parody of the self-parodying Norman Mailer. Here, for example, was Ali describing – through his medium, Richard Durham, of course – what it felt like to take a big punch from George Foreman:

55

'I must not get hit again. The tuning fork must stop vibrating. I must open the door of the room – the room I planned to take George into, the half-dream room. He has brought me here first. Only, I've been here before. I know about it. When I see masks and the actor's clothes hanging on the walls, the lizards playing saxophones and the bats blowing trumpets, I don't panic and run out. I put on actor's clothes. I go on the defensive.'

Lizards playing saxophones indeed! But I enjoyed reading the book for its more perceptive moments and I was especially interested by the suggestion that Ali's deliberate whipping up of public hostility against himself, his determination to be hated (as he was in America with a virulence that we, in Britain, would find hard to believe) generated a tidal-wave of mass-loathing which he continually resisted and defied and this unceasing effort of counter-aggression kept up a head of bellicose steam that rendered him virtually invincible against the individaul, limited aggressor in the opposite corner of the ring.

The other book, *Muhammed Ali* by Wilfred Sheed, was less interesting but still, in its way, readable. The author, I knew, had some reputation as a serious novelist and it was obvious from the start of his book on the life of the great boxer that he was not going to let anyone forget it. He might be writing about a popular sport but he would make few concessions to a thick-eared reader who might misguidedly pick up his study of the champion's career so, in the very early pages, he produced daunting sentences such as 'He [Ali] has exhausted the platonic possibilities of the heavyweight as celebrity'. A more serious flaw, however, was Sheed's essential ignorance of boxers and boxing. Ali, the public mythopoeic figure, was examined and anatomized at considerable length but the analyses failed to take proper account of one simple fact; the champion was interesting because he was a great fighter, a heavyweight who moved and hit with the speed of a fast welterweight, a brilliant and original tactician and a man of inexhaustible bravery, and, had he not been a great fighter, his antics outside the ring would have excited only irritation, boredom or pity. And when Sheed wrote on Ali's motivation as a fighter, 'fame was what it was all about', he showed in that shoddily-phrased comment he had no understanding at all of what it is that makes boxers take up the game. They always begin as amateurs, and the stem of that word 'amateur' is important: they start from love of the activity. That is why Ali started and that is why, with all the wealth, fame and every honour he could wish for, he would still go on fighting and would probably continue until, like the priest-king in the grove of Nemi, he would be slain and succeeded by a younger rival.

As January drew to its end the coldish weather changed to rain-lashed windy days and nights and then, dramatically, succumbed to a paralysis of snow and ice and frost. The air cut like grief, hurting the throat and making the eyes weep. When I walked across the road to the shops or the pub I moved slowly on the malicious surface, placing each foot carefully in front of me like an infant learning to walk or, more accurately, like a very old man. Twice I had to cancel visits to Culham College because the engine of my van refused to start. The central-heating of the flat was efficient, and I was thankful for it, but it seemed to make the air heavy and stifling and I felt continuously lethargic and vaguely depressed. I stayed in bed, often until noon, and I could not find the energy to do more housework than was strictly necessary. Mail continued to arrive in scarcely reduced quantities and the effort of dealing with it left me with no inclination for more work. I wrote letters, conscientiously made a daily entry in my journal or diary, and read desultorily. More snow and sleet fell. The days were dark from morning to evening and electric lights burned permanently in the shops, shining softly through the mist, elusively nostalgic, teasing the memory with hints of regret.

Three young men from Oxford wrote to say that they proposed starting a magazine and they needed '... advice on printing, costing and financing'. I wrote back and told them that I knew nothing whatsoever of these matters but, if they wished to be put in touch with potential contributors, I could supply them with the names and addresses of writers who might be prepared to help. Another correspondent wrote: 'About three months ago I came back from Americia [sic], Mexico and Honduras and I want to very much put down on paper my experiences in eight months traveling [sic] in thease [sic] countries with perhaps trying to get the book published when its [sic] compleated [*sic*].' I suggested, as tactfully as I could, that he would do well to take some kind of course in English grammar and composition before he thought of trying to write a book. I suspected that he would be affronted by this advice and was not surprised to hear nothing further from him.

There were invitations to read and talk about poetry at Ruskin College, the Oxford Writers' Circle and various schools in the area and a fairly thick wad of poems from a lady called Anna who, in the accompanying letter, implored me not to spare her feelings when criticizing the poems but give a totally honest opinion, even if it should be woundingly dismissive. I put her manuscripts to one side for more careful reading and opened the last evelope. It was a letter from Lincoln Kirstein.

Not long before moving to Berinsfield I had checked and returned to the publishers the proofs of a book I had written on poetry of the Second World War, *Not Without Glory*. Among the poets whose work I had discussed was an American, Lincoln Kirstein, who had served as an enlisted man in the US Army and published a collection of poems called *Rhymes of a PFC*. This book is something of a literary curiosity. It was published in 1964 and was very favourably reviewed by W. H. Auden in *The New York Review of Books* but it has never found a publisher in England and its author has received little public recognition, even in his own country. As Auden said in the review (which has been reprinted in *Forewords and Afterwords*) it was extraordinary that a book of such merit could be turned down by publisher after publisher and eventually find its way into print only because Kirstein himself could afford the expense of publication.

One of the reasons, as Auden acknowledges, is that Lincoln Kirstein is internationally famous as an impresario, General Director of The New York City Ballet, and he was instrumental in bringing the choreographer, George Balanchine, to the States to work with his Company. 'An impresario,' Auden states, 'is, by definition, someone who does not himself "create"; should he, by any chance, produce a work of his own, one assumes that it must be the trifle of a dilettante, unworthy of serious attention.' But, while this is quite true, I feel that there is another and more interesting reason for the general refusal to take Kirstein seriously as a poet: his work is dazzlingly original but its originality is not of a kind to impress the advocates of novelty and 'experiment'. All of his poetry is written in regular metrical forms of great variety; he employs patterns of strict rhymes and he has clearly learnt a great deal from such conservative English poets as Hardy, Kipling and Betjeman. His originality lies not only in that he has succeeded in Americanizing these seemingly intractable British voices and producing from them a uniquely individual voice of his own, but that he is able to explore, deeply and with power and sympathy, areas of experience that few other writers have penetrated. In *Rhymes of a PFC* he writes about the common soldier's experience of fear, loneliness, his hungers and dreams; he is fascinated by the interrelation of sexuality and physical terror, death and the orgasm, and he deals with such treacherous material with superb skill, a wit and an expert wire-walker's nonchalance and style.

I was very lucky in being able to borrow a copy of the *Rhymes* from the poet Gavin Ewart, and I devoted more space to my examination of Kirstein's work than to any of the other Second World War writers whom I dealt with in the American section of my book. Since I had quoted copiously from his poems my publishers were obliged to communicate with him in order to obtain copyright clearance. Evidently Kirstein was pleased with what I had written about him for he sent me a very friendly letter in which he made it plain that his feelings and ideas about poetry were similar to my own. Of the poetic situation in the United States he had written: 'Here, as far as most poets go, they only write for each other (which is different from writing, like Hopkins or Emily Dickinson, who wrote for themselves). "Poets" here qualify themselves by their "sensibility"; they are easily pleased and take no trouble in exploring the media of metric, rhyme or style. They just write, in a long drool, of sensed phenomena deeming whatever happens to or at them is worthy of print. There is no use trying to write about this, or complain, or indeed consider it. It's a fact of nature, like a drizzly day.'

Now, on that jaundiced winter's morning I unfolded Kirstein's latest letter and read that he expected to be in London early in the spring and hoped that we would be able to arrange a meeting. In the course of some dispirited observations about the state of contemporary letters he wrote: 'I cannot imagine how and why "poets" have abandoned the

59

marvellous tool of English metric, the richest of any language I know (only French, German and Italian). Balanchine assures me, and Vladimir Nabokov corroborates, that Pushkin is a marvellous virtuoso, and when I hear Balanchine recite from memory whole pages of *Evgeni Oneguin* it sounds more wonderful than Byron whom he's often considered to be like; he's not, either metrically or temperamentally; a far more profound imagination. Wystan Auden has, as you doubtless know, no use for the French – except Baudelaire – and he horrified Edith Sitwell once by saying, 'My dear, the Frogs simply have *no* poetry of interest: all sensibility, no notions.' He was, though, rather respectful of Valéry, and he said some nice things about St John Perse who, for me, writes the boring prosy rhetoric extended from Claudel.'

I shared almost all of Kirstein's views and it was good to know that someone whose poetry I admired and whose intelligence, learning and experience of many worlds were patently considerable, should give support to my grimly held beliefs about poetry, grimly because I knew that many sophisticated critics would regard them as untenably naive. I am unrepentant. 'Why,' as Kirstein said, 'abandon the marvellous tool of English metric', and, really, no poet of real accomplishment has ever done so. The poetry that is, for me, unassailably great, the poetry that I repeatedly return to with ever increasing pleasure, is all of it constructed to some metrical pattern and, furthermore, the genuinely innovatory, the truly 'experimental', is always firmly rooted in the achievement of the past. So much of what is called 'experimental' literature, in both verse and prose, is surely misnamed. The word 'experiment' derives from 'experimentum' – 'that which has been experienced' – and what, for the writer, has been experienced is the work of his great predecessors. The truly experimental poets are not those eccentric and often ill-informed novelty-mongers who would abandon the firm ground of the achievements of the past for the quicksands and wildernesses of an illusory freedom, those makers of sound-poems, found-poems, concrete poems and the like: the real experimentalists are and must be, steeped in the work of their eminent forebears; they are traditionalists like Hopkins, Hardy, Joyce, Eliot and Pound. 'No *vers* is *libre* for the man who wants to do a good job,' wrote Eliot, and I can think of no poet worth a light who, in his practice or theory, would contradict the author of 'The Waste Land'.

I do not mean, of course, that every poem that is any good conforms to a prescribed metrical pattern which is measured by accent. There are in the English language some very fine poems which would defy this kind of scansion. Christopher Smart's magnificent 'Jubilate Agno' is one; Whitman's 'Song of Myself' is another, both influenced by Hebraic psalm rhythms and parallelisms; and, in our own century, D. H. Lawrence found it necesary to move away from traditional accented verse to a more flexible measure based on quantity or duration. He wrote in a letter to Edward Marsh: 'I think I read my poetry more by length than by stress – as a matter of movements in space than footsteps hitting the earth...I think more of a bird with broad wings flying and lapsing through the air, than anything, when I think of metre... It all depends on the *pause* – the natural pause, the natural *lingering* of the voice according to the feeling – and it is the hidden *emotional* pattern that makes poetry, not the obvious form... it doesn't depend on the ear, particularly, but on the sensitive soul...'

Successful free verse of Lawrence's kind is rare and almost all of the poetry in English that gives me the most delight and nourishment is written in more or less conventional metres or, as in the case of 'The Waste Land', is is possible to trace the metrical substructure from which the verse never entirely breaks away.

Kirstein's letter had set me thinking about these matters when I remembered that Trevor, the man who had written to me from Buckinghamshire, was bringing his poems that evening. Perhaps I would be able to discuss with him some of these questions to our mutual advantage.

While I was waiting for Trevor to arrive I read through Anna's manuscript poems which had come that morning. The writing was literate but that was about all that could be said in its favour. Kirstein would not have enjoyed them at all. My guess was that she had read nothing outside of a few avant-garde magazines and maybe one or two paperback moderns. Her poems were very private, drawing much of their imagery from dreams, real or fictitious, surrealistic, vaguely morbid,

61

rhythmically moribund, their shape determined, it seemed, by the typographer's whim. And, like all such stuff, it was self-regarding, narcissistic and very boring. I put the poems to one side and promised myself that I would write to her the next day. Trevor arrived at seven o'clock, carrying a neat little attaché-case. He was a strongly-built man, rather above average height, with a healthy open-air complexion, enviably clear eyes and slightly greying hair. I guessed that he was in his mid forties. He wore a tweed coat, rather like a Norfolk jacket, and thick countryman's trousers of a darker tweed and unfashionable cut. His eyes had a look of candour, a sort of innocence you hardly ever see in city faces, but there was nothing bovine there: I thought I could detect intelligence and, possibly, humour. But there was a vulnerability in the face, something nervous and un-sure about the mouth which had a curious softness in the otherwise rugged setting. Not that he appeared outwardly to lack confidence. He showed none of the diffidence that my other visitors, who had come to discuss their literary ambitions and achievements, understandably often betrayed. He introduced himself, shook my hand firmly and hoped that he was not too early. Not at all, I assured him, and asked if he would like a can of beer. He refused this but accepted coffee. I helped myself to a MacEwen's Export and we sat down at my working table.

He said, 'Perhaps I'd better tell you a bit about myself to start with. I work on the land. Used to be a farm-manager but I was ill. Had a bit of a nervous breakdown as a matter of fact. I'm doing a general farm-hand's job now.' His accent was difficult to place: I found out later that it had originated in the valleys of South Wales but had been considerably modified in the Vale of Aylesbury.

I said, 'What caused the breakdown. Any idea?'

'No, not really. Overwork maybe. Worries I didn't know about myself, you know, subconscious worries, anxieties. Something like that. One day I was all right and the next I was gone. Looking back I can see – well, I *think* I can see – it was building up. But I didn't see it then. It came down on me like a landslide. I was buried. That's just over eighteen months ago.'

'How long were you in hospital?'

'Nearly a year.'

'And you're okay now?'

'Yes, I'm all right. Well, once a thing like that's happened to you, you're never exactly the same again. But I don't think it could happen again. I reckon I'd spot the warning signals.'

'You married?'

'Yes. My wife was great. I mean when I was ill. She still is. She didn't panic or complain or anything.'

'How did you manage when you were in hospital? For money, I mean.'

'She's got a job. She's a teacher. Clever. More educated than me. Just as well now I'm not earning so much. But we've got a cottage, goes with the job. We're all right. Can't grumble.'

'And you're writing poetry.'

'Yes. That's why I told you about the breakdown. I started then, when I was getting better. Never written anything in my life before and I suddenly found myself doing these poems. Lots of time on my hands – that's something I wasn't used to – and I suppose I was trying to make sense out of things. For myself, I mean. Trying to see if there was a meaning, a sort of pattern.'

I thought of Robert Frost's phrase about the poem being 'a momentary stay against confusion'. Trevor opened his case and brought out an alarmingly thick wad of manuscript.

'You probably won't think much of them,' he said cheerfully. 'I'm not a literary man really. I'm a primitive.'

That struck me as a decidedly unprimitive comment, but, when I began to read his poems, I quickly realized that it was a just one, and I guessed that it was a label which had been attached to his work by someone else – possibly his better-educated wife, the schoolteacher – and he had produced it in my presence with mixed intentions, partly to impress, but also to forestall technical or academic criticism which he would consider irrelevant to his kind of writing.

The first three or four poems were pieces of natural observation written in thumping metres with heavy rhymes, the demands of sustaining which had often forced him to employ weird syntax, clumsy inversions and archaisms, yet there was something impressive there, an honesty about his own feelings and, more important, a sharp clarity and precision of physical detail. There was a kind of authority that came from the fact that he really knew and loved the birds, animals, plants and trees he wrote about. They were a part of his world, and a valuable one, and his familiarity with them was at least as close as mine with my favourite books. I was reminded of John Clare,

63

but I soon discovered that Trevor had not heard of the Northamptonshire poet nor of any author whose name I mentioned. He was not in the least embarrassed by his ignorance of literature; on the contrary, I suspected that he was rather proud of it and I wondered if there had not been a note of complacency in his voice when he had announced that he was a primitive. I went on reading.

Some of the poems were less effective than the ones of direct perception: they were too full of abstractions and moralizing and he seemed to have little idea about which of his own writings possessed merit and which were frankly awful. When I suggested that a certain line or phrase or even a single word might be changed for the better he listened – or, rather, politely pretended to listen – then hastened on to direct my attention to the next poem. But when I gave up attempting critical judgement and handed each sheet of paper back with vague noises of approval he promptly became suspicious and said, 'But isn't there anything wrong with it? I mean, it can't be perfect, can it?'

So I would say something like: 'Well, this sounds – what? – a bit over-familiar? "White as a sheet." I seem to have heard that a few times before. And anyway it's not really accurate, is it? That's the trouble with clichés: they're not only bad because they're clichés but they're almost always lousy figures of speech too. And here you've got "hollow caves". Aren't caves necessarily hollow? You don't really need the adjective, do you? And if you've put it in just to fill out the line I'm afraid that's not good enough. Ideally, every single word in a poem should be absolutely indispensable...' And Trevor would nod courteously, absently, and say, 'What about the next one, then?'

I felt frustrated, irritated and oddly guilty. I did not know what he expected of me and I doubted if he knew either. The man was a poet, I felt sure of that. He was extraordinarily observant and sensitive to correspondences, and the language he used, while sometimes painfully strained and at times absurdly old-fashioned, showed that he took pleasure in the sound and shape and texture of words. And he really had subject-matter that was important to him. Every poem was about something; none was written from the wish to make a verbal artefact and you felt that each had been written because he had been taken by his theme and forced into speech or song. Yet even the best of them were too clumsily made and they all used idioms too remote from any speech recognizably of this century to be acceptable to an editor.

When I tried to explain this to him he looked at me with a half-smile that seemed both to accuse and forgive. I knew by then that it would be a waste of breath to advise him to read, say, the Thomases – Edward and R.S. – with whom I had at first believed he would feel some affinity. But now I knew he felt no need to read poetry at all. He was a writer, not a reader of the stuff. There was a kind of gentle but intransigent arrogance in the man, a barmy confidence in his own gifts. I had no wish to shake that confidence but when he asked, as I feared that he would, how should he set about getting his work published, I could not lie to him. I tried again, in the simplest possible terms, to explain that the poetry of any given era must reflect the rhythms and speech-patterns of the spoken language of the day, but I knew that he was not listening. He nodded, his eyes unfocused, and when I had finished he gave that half-smile, that gently reproached me for my betrayal, and said that perhaps he should be on his way.

It was about ten o'clock when he left. I saw him out into the street where he had parked his car. He opened the passenger's door and carefully placed his attaché-case of poems on the seat.

I said, 'I'm sorry if I haven't been of much help.'

Again, in the light of the street-lamp, that maddening and slightly mad smile of a man who has been unforgivably insulted but has no intention of retaliating. He nodded but made no answer. Then he got into his car and drove away. I went across to The Berinsfield Arms for a much-needed jar and some welcome unpoetical company.

FOUR

I WOKE UP ON THE DAY after Trevor's visit and saw through the bedroom window that the morning was grey with rain and mist. I got up, bathed and shaved, made some coffee and sat in the kitchen to go through my mail. There was not so much as usual and no manuscripts, thank God, though there were three invitations to give readings. Beyond the steamed-up window I could hear the rain hissing softly like escaping gas and it was probably this association that made me feel I was being slowly poisoned by my circumstances. In the three months I had been in Berinsfield I had written nothing except the review for *The Sunday Times*, countless letters and the daily entry in my diary, scarcely a satisfactory line of verse, nothing to give me the slightest sense of fulfilment. The idea behind the awarding of Fellowships and appointing Poets-in-Residence seemed, in theory, excellent: the writer would have certain duties to perform but, for a given period, he would be relieved of financial anxieties, supplied with accommodation and given plenty of opportunity to get on with his own work. And, although more of my time was absorbed by travel and giving readings and talks, dealing with correspondence and conducting private interviews than I had been originally led to expect, I could not justifiably protest that I was deprived of the leisure in which to think and write. Lack of time was not the problem.

The trouble was that I was living in an artificial environment. Berinsfield was one of the last places in the country that, given freedom of choice, I would have elected to live. My presence was unwanted; I had no socially useful function to perform, or none that would be recognized by the people of Berinsfield. They did not want me and I did not want them. No doubt the situation I was in would not have been unproductive for some writers: the solitary, self-sufficient author, whose work was primarily concerned with ideas, would almost certainly welcome the isolation, and the indifference of his neighbours to his aspirations; the neutrality, the hostility even, of his surroundings could be positively liberating, but, for better or for worse, my own writing had always been rooted in and fed by the life about me, my relationships with others, the loves, hates, and irritations and delights of living with other people and, virtually cut off from all this, I was adrift, lost and impotent.

I tried to shake off the weight of gloom that hung on my spirits like chains. I washed up the few dishes that needed doing and then forced myself to write acceptance to the letters I had received that morning. Then I looked again at Anna's poems, but the more I read them the less I liked them. In a sudden fit of ill-temper I grabbed a sheet of paper, stuck it in the typewriter and wrote to her that I could see no merit at all in these formless pieces of writing and that she should either set about finding out something of the craft of verse or take up some less demanding activity. I read through my note and screwed it into a ball and threw it away. No point in venting my bad temper and frustration on her. I put her manuscripts away and told myself that, later on, I would think of a kinder way of returning them.

That afternoon I went to a College of Education a few miles from Berinsfield and read to a group of students, all of whom were studying English Literature as their principal subject. They listened attentively enough, and when the time came for questions they showed no hesitation in speaking up but, as I had learnt to expect, their ignorance of books in general, and poetry in particular, was formidable. Authors, whose names at least one would have thought to be household words, proved to be quite unknown to them. It appeared that they read little or nothing beyond the few works prescribed the syllabus, and one young lady expressed surprise to learn that Thomas Hardy had written poetry as well as novels and a very brief exchange with her established that her knowledge of Hardy's fiction was not extensive: in fact, she had actually read *Tess of the D'Urbervilles* and she had seen the film of *Far from the Madding Crowd*. Another student needed to be told that blank verse and prose were not the same thing and his girl-friend advanced the view – one that seemed to receive a good deal of support among her peers – that my old-fashioned harping on technique was to be deplored on the grounds that it prevented spontaneity and sincerity. I left the college more depressed than when I had arrived.

In the evening I went to the Club for drinks with Brendan and Jack.

Brendan said, 'Oh, before I forget. What you doing tomorrow?'

'Tomorrow? Saturday, isn't it? Nothing particular.'

'Listen. Mel's fighting in the Home Counties ABA's at Hitchin. Feel like going?' I'd like you to see the boy have a go.' He grinned. 'And I wouldn't mind a lift in your van.'

I said that I would very much like to go.

'Good. I've got us a couple of tickets. They fight off the semi-finals in the afternoon. We'll get there about seven for the finals. No need to hurry it. I'll call for you about half-four. We'll be able to get well on the way and maybe stop for a jar. Okay?'

'Okay.'

I asked Jack if he wanted to come but I was not surprised when he said no. Boxing was not in his line.

The following day we set off in the van, driving through Thame and stopping in Aylesbury at opening-time for a couple of drinks in The King's Head. I had lived in Aylesbury from the age of nine to eighteen when I had left home to join the army at the outbreak of the war. I remembered the pub very clearly, as well I might for I had served much of my drinking appren-ticeship there, but I felt no nostalgic affection, either for The King's Head or for Aylesbury itself. The place had few happy associations for me and now that it had enlarged and become more industrialized what small charm it once possessed had evaporated. But when we were driving away in the van I was surprised by a tremor of remembered excitement and I recalled the days when I would travel in a hired coach with the Aylesbury and District Boxing Club to Letchworth, Slough, High Wycombe and various parts of London to do battle with the local young amateur pugilists; for a moment my nostrils were tickled by the smell of liniment, that pungent incense that must have issued from our gear and filled the coach, and I could faintly hear the songs we sang, 'You May Not Be an Angel', 'Pennies from Heaven' and 'Underneath the Arches'.

Brendan said, 'This is going to be Mel's year. Nobody to touch him. I want you to see him. He's a good 'un. Never takes a step back. Keeps throwing leather all the time. You'll see.'

I said I was looking forward to it.

We reached Hitchin just after seven o'clock, parked the van and made our way to the Town Hall where the Championships were being held. As we went into the building I noticed that Brendan's habitual slight swagger had become just a little exaggerated. He placed his feet down very deliberately, like a dancer, and this almost mincing gait was accompanied by a rhythmic sway of the shoulders, an alternate forward thrust like someone swimming the crawl though the arms were almost motionless by his side. His facial expression was fixed and impassive, the brow slightly furrowed as if with intense concentration. That was the fighter's mask. Brendan was acting a part, the ex-pug, veteran of a hundred bruising battles.

He said, 'Hang on a tick. I'll go and find out when Mel's on.'

He disappeared in the direction of the dressing-rooms and came back a couple of minutes later. There was a gleam of satisfaction in his eyes. 'He won his fight this afternoon. We'll see his final later on.'

'How did he win?'

'Points. The kid he's fighting tonight got a walk-over. Mel had a hard fight.'

'That's bad luck.'

'The luck of the draw. He'll be all right.'

We went into the hall. The crowd noise was loud and the canvas floor of the ring and the padded ropes were livid in the gush of radiance from the arc-lamps. Against the white brilliance tobacco-smoke was blue and wavering. Again excitement touched me, the old ghost of pre-fight tension, enough to tighten the stomach muscles and dry the saliva. The bout taking place came to an end as we found our seats. The Master of Ceremonies, fat and uncomfortable in his dinner-jacket, climbed laboriously through the ropes and the referee called the two boxers together in the centre of the ring and stood between them in readiness to raise the victor's arm when the verdict was announced.

Brendan said, 'Them's the featherweights. Mel should be on the one after the next. Light-welter.'

He lit a cigarette and dragged on it deeply. I knew that his nerves were pulled tight as the strings of a violin. Waiting to see someone who is emotionally close to you go into the ring is as agonizing as waiting to enter it yourself, indeed can be a good deal more so.

The next bout was closely contested and ended with a majority verdict for the boy who had shown the more aggression. A draw would have been a fairer decision but there are no drawn bouts in amateur boxing.

'Here he comes,' Brendan said.

Mel climbed into the ring. He looked pale, the shadows in the hollows beneath his cheekbones were dark, though that might have been a consequence of the harsh lighting. He rubbed his feet in the resin then jogged around in his corner, occasionally jabbing at the air, keeping his back to the other corner which was now occupied by his opponent who, when he shed his robe, showed that he was more heavily muscled than Mel, perfectly built for a boxer, with wide shoulders and lean but strong-looking thighs and calves.

The MC introduced the boxers and the referee called them together for the ritual touching of gloves and the muttered instructions: 'Let's have a nice clean fight, boys. Break when I say break and no ducking below the waist. Punch with the knuckle part of the glove and watch your heads. Back to your corners and come out fighting.'

A few moments later the time-keeper called, 'Seconds out the ring! First round!' and the bell clanged. The fight was on.

I had watched Mel shadow-boxing, punching the bag and skipping, but this was the first time I had seen him in serious action. It was obvious, almost from the first blow struck, that he was hopelessly outclassed. As Brendan had said, he never stopped coming forward, but none of his punches was connecting and he was walking into jabs and hooked counters that jolted his head so far back that he would have been looking straight up into the lights if he had been looking anywhere. Courage he had in abundance but, on this showing, no idea of ringcraft and no tactical sense at all. He plunged forward, throwing swings and hooks that were evaded or blocked with ease and his adversary's gloves thudded into his face and body in an endless tattoo. I heard Brendan groaning and swearing by my side and I wished I were anywhere but in that damned arena.

Mel lasted the distance, though I thought that a more humane referee would have stopped the bout before the end of the second round when it had become obvious that Brendan's son was not going to land one of his by then weary and almost perfunctory swings. After the decision had been announced and the boxers had returned to the dressing-rooms Brendan said, 'Let's go for a drink.'

There was a bar in the hall but it was crowded so we went out to a pub.

Brendan took a long pull at his Guinness. Then he said, 'Bloody women. That's the trouble with him. He's been with the bloody birds. You could tell. He was shagged. Right from the start. Weak as a kitten. Never seen him like that before. Hardly lift his hands. Couldn't bust a wet paper bag. Terrible! Terrible!'

'Maybe he was over-trained. A bit stale. He looked –'

'Over-trained! Over-bloody-strained, you mean. On the job. Too much of the old one-two. A bloody disgrace. If I've said it once I've said it a thousand times. You can't do both. He deserved all he got. I was ashamed of him.'

I knew that Brendan's rage was a screen for the bitterness of his disappointment. I thought that Mel had looked sluggish, almost somnambulistic, in the way that very stale fighters look, or those whose nervous tension has drained them of all their stamina before the first bell has sounded. I suspected that Mel was the kind of boxer who goes through hell in the hours of waiting to enter the ring. I felt sorry for the boy and I felt sorry for Brendan, but there was nothing I could say to help either of them. We had another drink and went back to the hall. Brendan visited the dressing-rooms to see his son and I returned to my seat. When he rejoined me he said, 'Mel's going back with the trainer. We'll watch a couple more fights and then head back, if that's all right with you.'

It was all right with me. A couple of strong but not very skilful middleweights swapped punches with enthusiasm for three rounds and then we saw a quick knockout in the light-heavyweight final.

'Might as well stay for the last fight,' Brendan said and afterwards I was glad that he had made the suggestion for the heavyweight final had the effect of dispelling or at least mitigating his despondency over Mel's ignominious defeat.

There was a sudden ripple of interest in the crowd as the big boys approached the ring and then some guffaws and jeers as the boxers ducked between the ropes and went to their corners. One of them was a medium-sized heavyweight of about six feet or a little over, weighing about fourteen stones but carrying too much of it around the waist. His opponent outweighed him by at least three stones, a large proportion of which was centred

71

round his ample stomach which bulged like an alderman's. He was a negro with a startled Afro hair style. The gloves looked strangely shrunken at the ends of his beefy arms. I saw that the white boy was taking nervous looks over his shoulder at the huge black and he looked distinctly apprehensive. I guessed that he was a novice and that he was wishing that he was elsewhere.

'Hey, will you just look at that gut,' Brendan said with awe. 'Have you ever seen anything like it?'

When the bout started, my suspicions that the white boy lacked experience were at once confirmed. His stance was stiff and awkward and he leaned back from the waist, a certain sign of a frightened novice, and he backed away, pawing out with a left lead which, had it ever touched his opponent, would have done so as an avuncular pat on the head rather than a proper punch. The black boy was no more experienced though noticeably less apprehensive. He advanced, brandishing his gloved fists in the air like a couple of primitive clubs, threatening terrible violence but accomplishing nothing. After a few moments of white retreating and black coming forward with vaguely threatening gestures, and the crowd roaring more and more loudly their amusement and derision, the white boy suddenly held his ground and essayed a ponderous round-arm-swing with his right fist. It hit his aggressor smack on the nose. The corpulent black boy took a pace back, dropped his hands to his side and glared with outrage at his cruel assailant, who promptly hit him again. This was too much. Black blundered forward, seized white by his shoulders, pulled him violently towards his own curly head which came down to crack into the centre of the white boy's face in the fiercest and most flagrant butt I have seen outside the Glasgow Gorbals. White staggered back with a bleeding nose and an expression of pain and disbelief and the referee led the black boy to his corner and disqualified him. Brendan roared with helpless laughter and was still chuckling when we reached the van.

I told him that I was feeling tired and suggested that he should drive back to Berinsfield. He liked to drive and had no car of his own so, as I had expected, he was happy to take over the wheel and the business of driving helped to keep his mind off Mel's performance, though at intervals on the journey he would give a sudden groan and curse the debilitating effects of sexual

72

indulge on strong young fighters who never took a pace back.

'I'll have him working tomorrow,' he said. 'I'll get the young bugger fit. I'll give him birds. He'll win that ABA title next year. I'll see to it he does. Honest, Vernon, you wouldn't know he's the same boy you saw tonight as the one I know. Honest to God, he'd have eaten that kid tonight if he'd been fit. I've seen him put better lads than that away, no bother. Bloody women. I'm telling you, that's what was wrong. He'll be different next time. You wait and see. He'll be a different boy, I promise. Made me look a fool. You'll be thinking I'm daft or something, going on about how good he was. I know he was terrible tonight. Terrible! I was ashamed of him.'

I said, 'Everybody has an off-night.'

Brendan grunted.

When we got back to Berinsfield Brendan dropped me at the flat and drove on to his own home. He would bring the van round the next morning, he said, just before twelve. We could have a couple of jars.

Why not.

During the next two or three weeks much of my time was taken up by poetry-readings, I found that I grew steadily less eager to embark upon the next one. Most of the school visits were at least tolerable and some of them positively enjoyable; my experiences of two junior schools, one at Mortimer and the other at Cholsey, near Wallingford, left me exhilarated and convinced for the moment that I was doing a useful job. In each of these schools the Headmaster and his staff were devoted to the children who seemed refreshingly free of any prejudices about poetry and the teachers were not disposed, as so many are, to make preposterous claims on behalf of their pupils' attempts to write original poetry of their own.

I was once asked to give a reading at a residential course for teachers of English organized by the Department of Education and Science and held at a provincial university. The main concern of the course was with children's 'creative writing' and the teachers were instructed, through lectures, seminars and discussions, in the various ways to stoke the creative fires in their young charges and many of them had brought along 'poems' by their little students which were pinned up on the walls of the principal lecture room. My own presence there was apparently intended to provide a relaxing hour in the evening after the day's serious work; in other words my role was seen by my hosts as primarily that of entertainer. The man whose task it was to introduce me was a member of Her Majesty's Inspectorate of Schools, an expert in the teaching of English to infants and juniors. He began his introductory remarks by twinkling roguishly at the audience and saying, 'Well, we've been talking about and reading a lot of children's poetry over the past few days and some splendid work we've seen, too. And now, this evening, just to show that some grown-ups are also capable of writing the stuff, we have…'

No doubt he was aiming at a note of levity to put the audience at its ease, but what he said annoyed me and I refused to let it pass.

'I do realize thay you're all teachers,' I told the assembly, 'and I know that you've got a difficult job. All the same, I get a bit tired of hearing about the marvellous "poems" written by eight-year-olds. Very young children do not write poems and they never have done. I can see that you've got to call what they write by some name and it's all right, I suppose, to call them poems as long as you understand that you're using the word as a convenient label and not as an accurate description. What children occasionally do is produce an occasional image, a line or a phrase that shows a freshness of vision, an unexpected combination of words that can surprise you and give you pleasure. But an image or a phrase or a line isn't a poem. A poem is the exploration and shaping of an experience. It begins, as Robert Frost said, 'in delight and ends in wisdom'. And to make a poem, a real poem, demands intelligence, imagination, passion, understanding, experience, and not least a knowledge of the craft. The reason why a few lines by a young child sometimes looks like a poem is because the young mind generally hasn't learnt to deal with abstractions. The child's likely to be concerned with the concrete, with things rather than ideas, so by accident he's more likely to come closer to writing a poem than the adult non-poet who mistakenly feels obliged to make big generalized statements about life, truth, freedom and the rest of it.'

74

'What about Rimbaud,' someone demanded, 'wasn't he a poet?'

'Of course he was a poet, but he wasn't a child. He was a monster, a monster of intellectual precocity. He was writing perfect Latin hexameters when he was fourteen. We're talking about ordinary little kids, not about Rimbaud or Pope or Chatterton.'

There was a restrained rumble of disapproval from the teachers and some very angry looks were thrown in my direction.

The Inspector cleared his throat. 'Ah well, yes, ah…an interesting point of view. Not one perhaps that you'll easily persuade us to accept here, but…ah…interesting…food for thought. And now perhaps you would like to…?'

Then I realized what an awkward position I had placed myself in. I could sense my audience straining at the leash, waiting to pounce on my pretensions as a poet and rip them to tatters. But good fortune and cowardice protected me. I had travelled that day by train and had brought with me John Hayward's *Penguin Book of English Verse* to read on the journey. I dug into my bag and brought this out and began with winning modesty to read some examples of real poems by real poets which I hoped would illustrate my contention that there was a world of difference between the complex and subtle organization of a work of art and an isolated and unambiguous moment of perception captured in words. Not, I added ingratiatingly, that I felt anything but admiring respect for their dedication and skill as teachers, nor that I regarded our apparent disagreement as more than a matter of terminology. By the time I had read some Donne, Herbert, Marvell, Crabbe, Browning and Yeats they were either mollified or stupefied and I fulfilled the terms of my contract by reading – without hostile audience participation – three of my own poems and then escaped as quickly as was consonant with good manners.

But, as I have said, the teachers at Cholsey and Mortimer were of a different kind from those who were afflicted by a kind of child-worship that I found especially puzzling in a group of people who daily encountered evidence of the infant ignorance it was their professed duty to alleviate. Some of the children from Cholsey subsequently sent me examples of their original writing and, while nothing I saw made me change my view of

75

child-writing, I was pleased and touched to receive them.

Less pleasant than my school visits was a talk I gave to a Writers' Circle. This took place in the house of one of the group's members. They were all women and most of them of a peculiar unattractiveness that I have come to associate with unpublished female authors: it was not simply a matter of their stout and ill-formed bodies, the double chins that sprouted little wiry hairs, the awful dresses like boarding-house wallpaper, but something about the eyes, the beady suspicion, the watchfulness that refused to be hoodwinked.

I talked for about forty minutes on the subject of writing in general, placing special emphasis on the necessity for truthfulness. Whether we are writing in prose or verse, I told them, we must never use language in a merely decorative way, that every qualifying word – every adjective or adverb – must be very carefully inspected and weighed before it is used, and we must ask ourselves if the word is precise, if it is truthful, if it is absolutely necessary. Unless the answer to all of these questions is unequivocally affirmative the word must be thrown out. We should never forget the physical nature of language: that the noun is the solid bone, the verb is the activating muscle, and the purely functional parts of speech – conjunctions, prepositions, relative pronouns and so on – acts as joints and ligaments, while those seductive and often treacherous qualifying words are the flesh, and they are indispensable, for without them we would build only a skeleton, but we must remember that too much flesh results in obesity and there is nothing more unpleasing and inefficient than flabby writing.

I talked about poetry and the poet's need to try to find his own voice; of the fact that every poet whose work could grip, whose images, in Auden's words, 'could hurt and connect', possessed – whether he employed traditional or more experimental means – a recognizable individual voice and that his poems carried the signature of this voice in almost every line. But it was impossible for a poet to fashion this voice deliberately by contrivance and experiment; it could not be discovered or simulated through the cultivation of an eccentric diction or prosody, or by the employment of regional speech rhythms and patterns. The unique tone was a consequence of the poet's rigorous search for truth, his absolute fidelity to the nature of the experience he was exploring. The true poet, in the exercise

76

of his art – though not, alas, in his life – was incapable of lying: the formality of his art, the exigencies of his craft permitted no gaps into which the lie could insinuate itself, and this was why the poet was of no use as a propagandist. He could not fake. He had no choice but to tell the truth, his truth. Then I read a few poems, which I hoped would illustrate what I had been saying, by poets as various as Pope, Housman, Dylan Thomas and Crowe Ransom and, feeling quite pleased with my efforts, I sat down and invited questions. A hand was raised by a lady who wore glittering, demoniac spectacles.

'What about markets?' she said.

'Markets...?' For a moment I was lost, and then I realized what she meant. 'Oh, yes well...of course we all want to see our work in print. But it does seem to me that writers who start with worrying about that have got things back to front. I mean, that's not really why we write, is it? Surely we start because of – well, because of the kind of thing I've been talking about. The business of publication isn't really my affair. I'm not an agent or publisher or editor. I don't think I've anything much to say about that side of the writer's business.'

The Writers' Circle glared at me, furious and cheated.

One of them said, 'You get your work published, don't you? You get paid for what you write.' There was no mistaking the tone of accusation.

'Yes, I get paid if the work's published. But that's not really why I write. I think I'd go on whether or not I was published or paid. I think I would. I hope I would.' I thought it might be a good idea to attempt to lighten the mood. 'Of course,' I said, 'I've been giving you my own personal view on writing. By no means everyone would agree with me. A very great author once said, "No man but a blockhead ever wrote, except for money".'

There was no discernible change in my audience's gloom, not even a polite recognition that a pleasantry had been attempted. I added weakly, 'I'm not sure how serious Doctor Johnson was when he said that.'

The first lady spoke again. 'Why is it that modern writers go on so much about sex and violence and all the horrible things in life? Isn't it because it's what the public wants? They do it because it sells.'

I said that I did not think that modern writers wrote about sex and violence any more than writers of the past had done – a glance at the works of Shakespeare and his contemporaries, Webster for instance, would show that they had not avoided either topic – and, speaking for myself, I did not regard sex as one of the horrible things in life.

Eyes grew narrower, lips tight. They could have guessed as much. The organizer made a perfunctory little speech of thanks and there was a grudging patter of applause but no softening in the watchful condemning eyes. I resisted the temptation to tell the sex-and-violence lady that her rejection-slip was showing and left the place with relief. The pubs were open, thank God.

But this was a particularly disagreeable occasion. By no means all of my public appearances were as unpleasant, and many were enjoyable. I read my own work at an Arts Centre in Abingdon and at the Old Fire Station in Oxford to audiences who seemed appreciative and whose questions showed a real interest in and knowledge of literature, but the sheer frequency of these events was becoming almost intolerably burdensome. As I have said before, the enjoyment of poetry, for me, is largely a private one and I generally find that listening to a public reading, however accomplished, adds nothing to the ideal voice which I listen to in my head when I read a poem on the page, and quite often it can actually distract. Also, a large part of my pleasure comes from seeing in detail how the poem is made, and for this I must have the artefact physically before me. I am aware that there are many people who enjoy listening to poetry being read aloud and even prefer to receive it in that way and I respect their preference without sharing it. I know poets who enjoy reading their work in public and I have sometimes enjoyed doing so myself, but even then my pleasure has been tinged with uneasiness, a feeling that what I was engaged upon was not what my true function should be, that the ambiguous rôle, something between the entertainer and the teacher with perhaps a touch of the guru, was something to be abjured.

I remember when public readings of poetry were rare, certainly any featuring younger poets of small popular reputation, and until the late nineteen-fifties I do not believe that I had given more than half-a-dozen performances in front of audiences. Then the situation changed suddenly and, it seems, irreversibly. I think it was in 1957 that the monthly poetry-readings run by Howard Sergeant and Alasdair Aston were started at The Greyhound pub in Dulwich and on one of the first, if not the very first, of these occasions I read with Ted Hughes and Patricia Beer to a large and enthusiastic crowd. From that time public readings became an increasingly demanding and profitable part of most poets' professional lives and now, with the establishment of such organizations as The National Poetry Secretariat, the literature section of the Arts Council of Great Britain and the various regional Associations, there can be scarcely any published writer of verse who has not been asked to read his work in different parts of the country and been paid an acceptable fee for doing so.

Of the many readings I have taken part in during the past twenty years or so the most interesting and pleasurable were the Jazz and Poetry Concerts organized by Jeremy Robson. It was, I believe, in 1962 that I was telephoned by an old friend, Dannie Abse, who said, 'How would you like to read at a jazz and poetry affair in Birmingham?'

My immediate reaction was to give an emphatic refusal. I had heard vaguely of the combination of jazz and poetry and imagined some subterranean cave, redolent with the fumes of hashish and loud with cacophonous noises being belted out by glazed-eyed trumpeters while a bearded hop-head intoned ungrammatical psalms in praise of his own genitalia.

Dannie said, 'All you do is read your poems just like any other reading.'

On reflection I realized that Dannie himself did not fit into my jazz and poetry vision.

'What about the jazz? When does that happen?'

'They play numbers in between the readings. Some of the readers do things with an accompaniment but I don't. You can please yourself. And the money's okay. I think you'd enjoy it. Tell you the truth, I was doubtful myself when Jeremy suggested it the first time, but it's all right. I was surprised. The musicians are great. You get huge audiences. You can sell your books. Give it a try.'

So I agreed to go, though I was still very doubtful. My taste in music was unadventurous. I loved Mozart, Beethoven, Brahms, Elgar and Sibelius and felt I was being rather daring when I listened to Stravinsky or Bartok. I knew nothing of jazz except for a few of the popular recordings of Fats Waller, Louis Armstrong, Benny Goodman and Duke Ellington, which I found pleasant enough, but I could not envisage anything I had heard being related to poetry. I was in for a surprise.

The jazz group on that first occasion was led by the pianist Michael Garrick, and featured Joe Harriott and Shake Keane. They were all fine musicians and excellent company and I am sure that none had ever taken any kind of drug stronger than a whisky. Furthermore they were intelligent men and responsive to poetry in a way that made me ashamed of my prejudiced ignorance of their art. Jeremy Robson was a quietly efficient impresario as well as one of the poets who produced work specially written to be read to a musical backing and, again, my prejudices had to take another bruising assault, for the combination of words and music proved most effective.

During the nineteen-sixties I took part in literally scores of poetry and jazz concerts in various parts of the United Kingdom and I recall those times with affection and slight incredulity, for it seemed that I had strayed from the familiar and comparatively sedentary world of the writer into the more raffish, nomadic and at least superficially more eventful world of the travelling entertainer. A lot of time was spent in travelling in cars, vans, trains and even aeroplanes. I remember being snowbound in Belfast, fogbound in Cambridge, boozed in Bangor, scarred in Scunthorpe, laid in Leicester, and almost always happy even when, as occasionally happened, the audiences were disappointing or the accommodation inferior.

Pleasant surprises as, for instance, when we were booked to appear at a small town in East Yorkshire. The concert was held in the local high school and it was well attended and received. The snag about this trip, or so it seemed to me, was that we – the musicians and the poets – were not to be accommodated in an hotel but scattered among volunteers who had offered hospitality in their homes. Dave Green, the bass-player, and I found that we were to stay with a schoolmaster and his wife. The jazz and poetry concerts generated a kind of atmosphere very different from the decorous mood of the purely literary occasion, and at the close of each performance those taking part were always ready for a few drinks to assist in the winding-down process. Since this concert was being held in a school there was no bar to repair to during the interval and, by the end of the evening, I was more than customarily anxious to find a pub and enjoy a pint of bitter. It was not to be.

Our host, a middle-aged teacher of mathematics, appeared

as soon as the last number had been played and told Dave and me that we must hurry because his wife had prepared a meal for us and already it was later than he had expected the concert to finish. He was obviously keen to get home as quickly as possible and my one, unhopeful suggestion that we might stop for a quick one on the way was either unheard or ignored. Dave and I exchanged melancholy looks of resignation and got into the car of the schoolmaster who asked us to call him Fred. I think that Dave shared my unkind impulse to call him something else. We were driven with pedagogic prudence to our destination, a semi-detached house a couple of miles from the school.

Fred's wife was called May. She was, like her husband, grey and unmemorable, but she was an attentive hostess in her own way and was much concerned lest the large meal of shepherd's pie, vegetables and thick gravy had been spoilt. It had not. We sat down at the table and ate. Conversation did not flow easily. Once Fred and May had discovered that we were both married and ascertained the numbers and sexes of our progeny there was one of those silences that throbbed with the frustrated effort of straining for suitable topics. Dave and I chewed stolidly at our shepherd's pie and if our gaze should chance to encounter that of host or hostess we would beam and nod and perhaps say, 'Very nice...mmm...delicious.' Dave could coax sustained and eloquent commentaries from his double-bass but, even in more propitious surroundings, he was no conversationalist. Words, he had evidently decided, were my business and he would leave me to do the talking for both of us.

I questioned Fred about the school and we managed to exchange a few banalities on education, youth, and the changes that had occurred in society since we were young. The main difficulty in maintaining any kind of meaningful interchange was that I had no knowledge of his speciality nor he of mine. Literature, it seemed, was as incomprehensible to him as mathematics to me and we could find no common ground between the two. He did not care for music but enjoyed sailing. I mentioned the cinema and theatre and he told me with quiet satisfaction that he had not visited either for longer than he could remember. By the time we had all finished eating and left the table to sit more comfortably with our coffee I was beginning to feel a curious numbness in the mind and throat as if I might not be able to speak again until I had left that house.

81

Then Fred, clearly desperate, said, 'You do any gardening?'
Dave and I shook our heads.

'Fred likes his garden,' May told us. 'Almost as keen on it as he is on his wine.'

For a moment I thought that my mind had broken under the strain. I blinked. 'Did you say…I thought you said wine.'

'That's what I did say. Makes marvellous wine, does Fred.' May smiled at her husband with the tolerant pride of a mother praising her young.

'Make wine, do you?' Dave said, making his longest speech of the evening. 'That's interesting.'

'Yes, a great hobby of mine. Been doing it for years. Make all kinds – rhubarb, dandelion, elderberry, cherry, parsnip, potato, marrow – oh, all kinds. You name it, I've made it.'

Dave and I swapped looks in which hope and disbelief were mingled.

I said, 'Is it…er…good? I mean, I haven't drunk home-made wine for years. I've forgotten what it's like.' I was aware of an ingratiating leer stuck on my face like a false nose.

'Would you like a glass now?'

'Ah, yes, yes I would. Very much.'

Dave nodded vigorously and made affirmative noises.

Fred left the room and returned a few seconds later carrying two bottles. His wife produced glasses and he filled three of them with pale amber liquid. May said that she would not have any because it gave her a headache and, anyway, she had to be up early in the morning, so would we excuse her if she cleared away the dishes and went to bed. Dave and I congratulated her again on the fine meal she had provided and made a token offer to wash up which was instantly declined. A little later she called, 'Goodnight,' adding whimsically, 'Don't drink too much of Fred's potion. It's strong stuff!'

'We won't,' we promised, holding out our glasses to be recharged.

'Well,' Fred asked, 'what do you think of it?'

I took another sip. 'Good. Very very good. What is it?'

'That's marrow.'

'Marrow? Good heavens, I'd never have guessed. It's delicious.'

He nodded, smiling, quietly self-congratulatory. 'Marrow. That was marrow. The first one you tried was parsnip. Hang on a tick, I've got something else you might like to sample.'

He went out of the room and came back with two more bottles.

We raised our newly filled glasses and drank.

'Wow!' Dave said.

'Well, what about that, then?'

'It's terrific. Glorious.'

'But what is it?' Fred asked. 'Can you guess what it's made from...'

I shook my head. 'I've no idea. I just know it's a lovely drink.'

'Dandelion.'

'Dandelion!' Dave echoed.

'Never,' I said, marvelling. 'You mean to say there's nothing in this except dandelions?'

'That's right.'

Dave said, 'Do you think I could try a tiny drop of the first one again? Just to compare them.'

'Wait a sec. In a minute. But just see what you think of this one.' Fred filled our glasses and his own from the fourth bottle.

All of the wines were palatable and all decidedly strong. Our earlier verbal restraint had not only disappeared but been replaced by something very close to its opposite. Even Dave was making his contribution to the talking. Very soon the four bottles had been emptied.

'You should try my potato,' Fred said with less than his usual clarity of enunciation.

'You should try mine,' Dave replied and we all guffawed at this robust sally.

Fred went into the hall and we heard him rummaging in the cupboard under the stairs where he kept his wine.

Then May called from upstairs in a frail, rather plaintive voice: 'Fred! Fred! Are you coming up, dear?'

He shouted back: 'Shan't be long, love! You go to sleep!'

His wife was continuing the discussion but her voice was cut off as if by a switch as he came back with more wine and shut the door behind him with a brisk back-heel kick.

And so another couple of hours or so passed pleasantly as the empty bottles proliferated and our talk became more inconsequential and less comprehensible. May had called two or three times, her expiring hope reflected in the dying fall of her voice, but by now she had given up and was probably fast asleep.

Another bottle was drained and Fred's expression suddenly changed from one of unfocused joviality to a kind of bemused cunning. He looked around the room warily as if suspecting the presence of hidden eavesdroppers. Then he said, 'Listen, boys. Before we call it a night I've a treat for you.' Again he traversed the room with his sidelong gaze. 'Listen.' His voice was lowered almost to a whisper. 'I've got some special stuff. It's been stashed away for six – no, I tell a lie – seven years. Seven years! You wait till you taste it. It'll be like nectar. Wine of the gods!' He tiptoed from the room.

Dave and I looked happily at each other.

'Just goes to show,' David said.

'You never can tell.'

'Never.'

We were both feeling the effects of the wine. The earlier exhilaration had given way to a sense of muzzy well-being and drowsiness was moving close. Fred seemed to have gone for a long time.

'What you think's happened to him?' Dave said.

'Maybe he's passed out.'

'Could be. I'm nearly ready for kip myself.'

Then Fred returned. One hand clutched a full bottle and the other was raised to his face, index finger laid perpendicularly at the side of his nose in an old-fashioned gesture of conspiracy. 'Got it,' he said. 'Sorry I took so long. It was under the floorboards.'

The wine was poured and drunk. By this time I don't think any of us would have been able to tell the difference between the rarest vintage and the most tongue-blistering hooch but we made appreciative noises and nodded sagely after each indelicate swig. Then it was time for bed. Dave and I were shown to our room and the next day we awoke to begin the long and painful journey through the hangover that waited to exact its toll for the night's wassail. Payment, we knew, was inescapable, but we agreed that the experience had been worth the price.

So many other memories of poetry-readings: the student at the University of Keele who expressed surprise that I should be reading that evening because, as he explained with more candour than diplomacy, he had always been under the impression that I had been killed in the First World War. Then there was an occasion, some time in the mid 'sixties, when Peter Porter and I gave a performance at The Midland Institute in Birmingham and when the time came for questions from the audience a neat demonstration of the failure in cultural communication between different age-groups was enacted. A young man asked us what opinion we held of the works of Dylan.

A good and original poet, Peter said, though one with certain obvious limitations. The uncritical adulation that had been accorded him shortly after his death, and the tendency, which was operative even in his lifetime, to mythologize the man had impeded a just evaluation of his work. I said that I thought some of the early poems like the one beginning 'Especially when the October wind' and 'Death shall have no dominion' had a permanent place in our literature but I could see no real development in his work. He was a poet who was infatuated or enchanted by a dream of innocence and he saw childhood as a pre-lapsarian state of consciousness, a paradise to which he constantly returned in his poetry, and it was this special kind of romanticism that gave to his work both the strength of its individuality and lyricism and the weakness of its immaturity.

The young man looked increasingly bewildered as Peter and I elaborated our views until someone in the audience called out, 'He doesn't mean Dylan Thomas, he means Bob Dylan!'

Oh.

We had no opinions on the achievement of the folk-singer, inevitably since neither of us had the least familiarity with anything he had composed.

Another, even more disconcerting incident occurred when I gave a solo reading at a ladies' society of some kind in Woking. Question time arrived and there was no response from my audience at all. I sat in uncomfortable silence for a minute or two and was about to fold up my poems and steal away when a lady rose to her feet and said in a loud and sensibly-shod voice, 'Why is it, Mr Scannell, that all of your poems sound exactly like prose?'

I had no answer except to apologize if this was indeed the case. I looked hopefully at the other ladies but none disputed their representative's verdict. So I left.

These few, slightly unusual recollections, comic or embarrassing, are the ones that return. The scores of pleasant occasions, when the audiences have been sympathetic and intelligently involved, tend to merge in the memory as a single event. I should be grateful for the opportunities I have been given to read my work in public; in fact, I am grateful and I hope that I have at least done poetry no real disservice. Any effort to stimulate interest in the art and encourage people to explore its richnesses more deeply must be applauded. But in Berinsfield my involvement in public performance was too continuous, too intensive, I needed longer periods for recuperation and contemplation between readings. Like a boxer who fights too often, I was becoming stale, losing my snap and eagerness and judgement; and I felt a guilty suspicion that I was likely to sell short myself, my audiences and, most important, poetry itself.

February, my fourth month in Berinsfield, drizzled to an end. I wrote letters, kept up the quotidian entries in my journal, but did little else. On the last day of the month an advance copy of my book on the poetry of the Second World War, *Not Without Glory*, arrived. It looked quite pleasing, I thought, from the outside. The dust-wrapper showed a reproduction of a photograph, lent by the Imperial War Museum, of a young soldier clutching an eighty-eight millimetre shell, his eyes staring ahead, unfocused, dulled yet profoundly miserable with the desolation of exhaustion and despair. This was the face of war, or more specifically of the Second World War as I had known it, the face of conscripted youth, ignorant, bewildered and trapped. It was not the face that everyone would regard as representative. There were, I knew, other and more acceptable, less accusing faces, those of the gallant young infantry officer and fighter pilot, the tough parachutist and commando, the older, sterner features of the General, the great Leader, resolute and unafraid. But this was the face of the lowest common denominator of the other-ranks, the Gunner, Private or Trooper who would never hold higher rank nor wish for it, the face of the unwilling sacrifice, stubborn, unimaginative and often, to his superiors, infuriating. And, looking at it now, over the long years, deeply pathetic in its immaturity. It was a good photograph. As for the contents of the book I felt almost unconcerned about them. It seemed a long time since I had completed the manuscript and there it was, for better or for worse, and there was nothing to be done about it.

It was not an ambitious book. I had written it because I had believed that, contrary to popular opinion, there was such a thing as a war poetry of the Second World War and that it was essentially different from, though not inferior to, the poetry of the Great War. Rupert Brooke, Wilfred Owen, Siegfried Sassoon and, perhaps to a lesser extent, Isaac Rosenberg, Edmund Blunden and Robert Graves were familiar names to anyone with the slightest acquaintance with twentieth-century English poetry, and the 'soldier-poet', along with the Unknown Warrior, No-man's Land, trenches, barbed-wire and poppies, was a permanent feature of the mythology of the War-to-end-Wars. But I found that, even among people who professed an interest in poetry, and in some cases were professionally concerned with it as teachers, that the best poetry written by men serving with one or other of the fighting forces in World War II was totally unknown or seriously undervalued. At a conference on Modern Verse, held at a provincial university in 1968, and attended exclusively by students specializing in English Literature, not one of them had even heard the names, far less read the work, of either Keith Douglas or Sidney Keyes, and I felt that this ignorance was not local but general and would be scarcely, if at all, altered today.

The difference between the poetry of the two wars had little to do with the formal changes manifested by some of the most influential work of the 'twenties and 'thirties, the post-imagist Modern movement, though I suspect that the reputation for charlatanism and obscurantism that Modern Poetry, along with Modern Art, had acquired among the philistines of all social classes by the outbreak of war was at least partly responsible for the almost total failure of the British press and public to recognize that 'war poetry' of merit was being produced. As late in the war as 1945 an anthology, *War Poems from the Sunday Times,* was published, and those contributors who could claim any reputation as poets were Laurence Binyon, Richard Church, Wilfred Gibson, Edward Shanks (the most solidly represented, with seven poems) and Sir John Squire, every one an Edwardian, all of them writing, with varying degrees of accomplishment, in a style and idiom which ignored utterly the changes which had occurred in art, literature, politics, language, thought and modes of consciousness since 1914. The two or three younger writers were no different from their elders and, understandably, none of their names would be recognized now by readers of contemporary poetry. Yet by the time that book was published, Alun Lewis, Sidney Keyes and Roy Fuller had each brought out two volumes of war poetry, and writers of the distinction of Keith Douglas, Henry Reed, F. T. Prince and Norman Cameron – to name a few – had contributed work to publications like *Poetry London, Penguin New Writing, Horizon, The Listener* and *The New Statesman* and had gained considerable reputation among their literary peers.

None of these poets could be called 'avant-garde' or in the least 'obscure'. Naturally, the language they employed reflected the syntax and cadences of the speech of their own time and each, in his different way, had profited from reading the major senior contemporaries, Yeats, Eliot, Graves and, much closer chronologically to themselves, but perhaps the greatest single influence on the best poetry of World War II, W. H. Auden. It was not their style or idiom that made them unacceptable, but their attitudes, for what the journalists were demanding when they asked – as they did from time to time – 'Where are our War Poets?' was just the kind of hortatory, sentimental fustian that *The Sunday Times* provided. They did not understand – and this was surely proof of invincible literary obtuseness – that, since this was a different war, fought by a different generation, speaking a different language, its poetry must also be different. But it was not poetry that they really wanted; it was propaganda, lenitive or inspiriting, presented in the familiar and undisturbing form of late romantic and early Georgian pastiche; they did not want the bleak and poignant records of conscripted man struggling to preserve his humanity and individuality from being crushed and transformed by the processes of military indoctrination, or subjective explorations of the interrelations of sexuality, physical fear and violent death. It is true that there were Second World War poems which presented accurate accounts of battle not unlike those of Sassoon and Owen, but, as in the case of Keith Douglas, the finest of the British poets, these were not protests or warnings like those of the poets of Flanders. Douglas was primarily interested in his art, by finding out how much of war experience could be assimilated and recreated by poetry, and he was fascinated by the metaphysical implications of living cheek by jowl with death.

The British poetry of the Great War supplies an accurate measure of the changes in the emotional temperature of those terrible four years. The early enthusiasm, patriotic fervour and sense of adventure at the prospect of an exhilarating and spiritually cleansing experience were celebrated, most notably though not of course exclusively, by Rupert Brooke's sonnets; then came the poetry of action, still enthusiastic and patriotic, poems such as Julian Grenfell's 'Into Battle'; and then the most memorable and probably the most lasting poetry of the war, the work of Sassoon and Owen and a few others embodying the sick disillusionment of the fighting man and protesting bitterly at the inhumanity and complacency of the real enemy, not the Germans but the politicians, profiteers and armchair warriors safe behind the firing line. Much of what they wrote was public poetry addressed directly to a particular audience, those at home who were duped by the lies of the journalists. 'All a poet can do today is warn,' said Owen. But the serving poets of the Second World War felt no need to broadcast warnings. The civilian population knew as much of the realities of war as they did. They had no disillusionment to express because they had cherished no illusions at the beginning. In the main their voices were private, self-communing, to be overheard rather than heard and their essential preoccupations were metaphysical.

I hoped that my book might do something towards directing the attention of younger readers, to whom the Second World War was as remote as the First and, as I have found, often confused with it, to a poetry which would tell them more exactly and movingly than any film or history book what it was really like to have lived through and served in that war. I knew only too well that I was no scholar and that *Not Without Glory* would probably seem amateurish to the professional academic critic. But at least, I told myself, I did know a bit about my subject. I had served through the war against Fascism and I had been seriously reading and trying to write poetry for thirty-odd years so I ought to be able to suggest a few helpful guide-lines to teachers and their students. I did not suspect then that I was in for a few surprises after the book's publication.

FIVE

WINTER HAD PASSED: it was March and I had completed half of my tour as Poet-in-Residence at Berinsfield. Bright sunlight, like a keen and smartly-attired young officer, inspected the gloom, dust and disorder of my flat and did not approve. I accepted its reprimand but did nothing to improve the place. Really, there was not much I could do and, in any case, I felt too lethargic to try. Spring had come again, *spring,* that sprightly, energetic word that had, for some years now, seemed to me to carry undertones of irony. 'In the Spring a young man's fancy lightly turns to thoughts of love' Tennyson wrote in 'Locksley Hall'; but what about the old or middle-aged man? For him there will often be a heartlessness in the vivid beauty of the season, in the birds' songs, the thrusting tulip and the yellow explosion of daffodils. The sense of optimism and expectancy, the promise of summer fulfilment, can be cruel to those who know that the future holds in its gradually opening fist only a one-way ticket to the City of Darkness. I remembered reading somewhere that more suicides occur in spring than in any other season. Easy to believe.

On March 4th I visited a comprehensive school a few miles outside Oxford to read and talk to the pupils. When I arrived, shortly before eleven o'clock in the morning, I was shown by the secretary into the Headmaster's study and was asked to wait there for a few minutes until the Senior English Master, who was busy teaching, was free to join me. The Head, unfortunately, was away attending a meeting. He had asked his secretary to apologize for his absence and tell me how much he regretted missing my reading. Headmasters, I had found, were often busy elsewhere when I visited their schools and they were always disappointed at being deprived of the pleasure of meeting me and hearing me read my poems.

I lit a cigarette but put it out after only a few moments; the tobacco was unfriendly to my dry and ashen mouth and I felt slightly dizzy. I had a hangover. There were a few books in the glass-fronted case: a paperback copy of *The Uses of Literacy,* Trevelyan's *Social History, The Concise Oxford English Dictionary, Lord of the Flies, The Hobbit,* some uniformly bound Dickens and a dozen works on educational theory and psychology. Not a poem in sight. By their books ye shall know them.

There was a knock on the door and the Senior English Master came in. He was a pleasant young man with that appearance of candour and irrepressible appetite for life that goes with youth, good health and an untroubled conscience. I felt sure that the symptoms of my hangover must be shamefully visible to his clear gaze.

He said, 'We've got a few minutes before we have to start. Just time for a cup of coffee. How would that suit?' He went out of the study and came back almost at once. 'Mrs Cope's fixing it for us. You'll stay to lunch, won't you?'

I had spotted a promising-looking pub on my way to the school and had mentally reserved a pint of bitter and a beef sandwich there at 12.30.

I said, 'It's very kind of you but I'm afraid I have to rush off. I've got an appointment in Oxford this afternoon.'

'Oh well. It's a pity from our point of view but maybe not from yours. I expect you've had your share of school dinners since you've been in Oxfordshire.'

The coffee was brought in. I tried another cigarette but it did not taste much better than the first.

My host said, 'Actually I've heard you read before. Some time ago.'

'Oh? Where was that?'

'Lancing.'

I had a vague recollection of having given a reading at Evelyn Waugh's old school quite a long time ago.

'Lancing? Did you teach there before you came here?'

He laughed. 'Good heavens, no! I was a boy when you came. Don't really remember much about it except being surprised when one of our masters told us you'd been a boxer.'

Senior English Master, and he remembered me visiting his school when he was a boy. My post-alcoholic depression darkened. He did not seem to notice. 'We've got a bit of a mixture of ages and ability-range here,' he said. 'But I expect you're used to that.'

I told him I was quite used to it. All I wanted was to get the session over as quickly as decently possible and reward myself with a healing pint and try to forget that I was old and faded and curling up a bit at the edges. But once I had started the reading I found the enthusiasm of my audience, their obviously

91

genuine interest, no longer mocking or threatening but temporarily palliative, and when the lunch-time bell sounded and the meeting was brought to a close I was surprised at how quickly the time had passed.

I did not linger over my beer and sandwich and arrived back in Berinsfield just before 2.30, in time for another drink before the pub closed and to buy a bottle of Spanish red wine. No more engagements had been made for that day so I planned to lie on the bed with Christopher Sykes's *Evelyn Waugh* and enjoy an idle afternoon. The hangover had quietened to an occasional faint whimper. Life, even at fifty-four, was not so bad after all.

Back inside the flat I washed up the dirty dishes that I had allowed to accumulate over the previous two days; then I uncorked the wine, poured myself a glass and carried it, with my book, into the bedroom. I took off my shoes and climbed beneath the coverlet and top blanket of the bed, arranged the pillows so that I could adopt a comfortable reading position, took a sip from my glass and opened the pages of my book. There was a gentle tapping on the outside door. I looked at my watch: twenty past three. Who could be calling at such a time? Both Brendan and Jack would be at work. The only person who had so far called without a previous appointment had been the vicar and nothing that had occurred at our first brief meeting had led me to expect another visit from him. Perhaps I had been mistaken about the noise and there was no one at the door. Then it sounded again, three taps, unemphatic yet unmistakable.

I put down the book, heaved myself off the bed, slipped my shoes on and went through my living-room into the hall and opened the door. A young woman stood there. The light was behind her so I could not see her face distinctly but I sensed rather than saw that she was unusually good-looking.

She said, 'Vernon Scannell?'

'Yes.' There was a slight and uncomfortable pause before I said, 'Won't you come in. It's not very...a bit scruffy, I'm afraid.'

She followed me into the living-room. Now that I could see her properly I saw that she was as attractive as I had at first guessed, or hoped; more so, perhaps. She was rather tall with straight dark brown hair worn long with a kind of carelessness that, judging from its opulent sheen, had taken time, skill and money to manage. Her eyes were large and very dark, juicy, eatable almost, like living grapes, and her mouth was full-lipped, generous. She moved with a kind of diffident grace.

I said, 'Sit down. I think that's the most comfortable...'

She did not sit but walked over to my book-case and began to look at the titles. This meant that I was facing her back.

I waited, but when she remained with her face to the books, not offering any kind of explanation of her presence, I said, "Would you like a glass of wine? Or a cup of coffee? I'm drinking wine. Spanish...Franco's Revenge.'

She continued, silently, to examine my books.

I went into the bedroom and came back with my wine.

She said, without turning away from the book-case to face me, 'Why didn't you send my poems back?' Her voice was very low, soft and warm, the colour of her hair.

'Your poems? Didn't I? I mean have I had...I'm afraid there's often a muddle. I'm not very methodical. And the Southern Arts people take their time sending things on to me. Maybe I've not had them yet.' She appeared to take no notice of this gabble. 'What's your name?' I asked.

'Anna.'

'Oh.' What the hell had I done with her poems? I remembered writing the ill-tempered letter of condemnation, thinking better of posting it and throwing it away. Her manuscripts must be in one of the drawers full papers that I constantly promised myself to arrange into some sort of order.

I said, 'I'm sorry. Of course I remember the poems now. I know I've been a hell of a time over answering. The trouble is I've had so much stuff sent me.' This was true but it suddenly sounded self-aggrandizing – the big man of letters being harassed by the demands of the small fry. I tried to correct the tone: 'I mean I'm a lousy correspondent at the best of times, hate writing letters, even to...' Christ, this was sounding worse, arrogant, off-hand, indifferent to my obligations as Resident Poet and to the feelings of those who wrote in the hope of receiving encouragement, help. If only she would turn round and look at me I would find the interview less difficult. I felt a spasm of irritation and an impulse to grab hold of her and swing her round to face me.

Instead I said, and I could hear the sharpness in my own voice, 'I asked you if you'd like a drink. Would you?'

Now she did turn away from the books but her head was lowered, eyes – from what I could see of them – downcast. She sat down, looked up briefly and said, 'I'll have some wine.'

I went into the kitchen and found another glass, filled it and topped up my own. Back in the living-room I handed her the wine and sat down at the littered table.

I said, 'I'm sorry. Matter of fact I did write to you about your poems.' She looked up quickly and down again, just enough to show derisive disbelief before she went back into hiding behind her expensive and beautiful hair. 'I did, really. But I didn't send the letter because I knew it wasn't any good. I hadn't said anything useful. Another thing. They're not the kind of poems I find it easy to say anything about.'

'Why not?'

'Well, for one thing they're very personal. It's all right for a poem to start from a private experience – most poems do, or a hell of a lot – but it must expand, it must grow outwards to touch other people's experience, it's no good if it stays dark and clenched and meaningless. It seems to me you're more concerned with your own states of mind and feelings than you are with writing poems.' She gave me a quick look again, ducking for cover before I could properly read it. I knew I was not making much of a showing. 'Look, I've got certain ideas about poetry, what it is, what it should be. For me. People who write about their dreams, or their own sensitivity or about very personal experiences that exclude other people's involvement, and when they write – as they nearly always do – in a kind of stuttering prose that's broken up into lines of uneven length for no reason that I can follow, people doing that kind of thing simply don't interest me. They're nearly always bores. Egoism on the scale they go in for is always boring. And you can't talk to them. You can't say,"I think you could have got this better, more clearly, sharper." You can't say that because you don't know what the hell it's supposed to be about anyway. You can't say, "The rhythm seems to falter here" because you can't see any rhythmic sense at all. And the language is usually so shoddy, so bloody careless and woolly that it can't be talked about. So, in the end, all you can say is, "If that's what you feel you must do, go ahead and do it. But please don't show it to me and don't kid yourself you're writing poetry. This kind of stuff oozes out. You don't have to work at it. It might give the writer some sort of relief but it doesn't do anything for the reader. The real poem is hard to write. You've got to work at it".'

'And you think mine are like that? Easy-oozy, shoddy, boring.'

I said, 'Look. You don't have to take any notice of what I've said. I might be wrong. About your work, I mean. I'll be honest: I didn't care for any of the ones you sent. But I'm so prejudiced against that kind of writing I might well be blind to real qualities that someone else would see and admire. I know I'm old-hat. But I'm not going to pretend to admire and enjoy something that leaves me cold.'

'Thanks.'

'No. I wasn't just thinking of your things.'

She said, 'What is it you're saying exactly? Everybody should write in metres and rhyme, stuff like that?' She seemed a little less inhibited and she kept her gaze on me for three or four seconds before her head went down again.

'No. Well, yes, something of the kind. Of course you don't have to use a regular metre and rhyme-scheme, but I think you ought to know how it's done. And why. It's all right using freer forms. Use free verse by all means if it's the best way, the only way, you can make your poem. But if you're writing in free forms because it's easier than sweating away at traditional forms, it won't do. And in fact, to do it properly, it's a damn sight harder. Learn your trade.' I was beginning to feel bored with my own voice and opinions. It seemed that I had said it all before so often that it had lost meaning. I said, 'What sort of poetry do you like? Who do you read?'

She shrugged. 'Poetry's not really my thing. I'm more into painting and music'

She looked up at me again and grinned. Her face changed disconcertingly. The rather sombre, Pre-Raphaelite aspect was suddenly transformed. She looked mischievous, almost *gamine*. 'I saw you come over from the pub,' she said.

'What?'

'I saw you come over from the pub. With the wine.'

'But that was…why didn't you stop me? It must have been – what? – nearly an hour before you knocked at the door.'

She grinned again and ducked her head. 'I was nervous.'

'How did you know who I was?'

Her head was still lowered. 'I saw your picture. On the back

95

of a book. Didn't look much like you. I mean you don't look much like the picture. A lot older.'

'Oh. I see.'

She gave a short grunt of laughter. 'Never guessed you'd look so old.'

I said, 'I only look old because I'm old.' I aimed at sounding flippant but it came out sulky.

She grinned again. 'Right.'

I finished my wine and replenished my glass, topping hers up and emptying the bottle.

'I'll find your poems.'

She said, 'No.'

'Don't you want to go through them?'

'No.'

'All right, then. But you'll want to take them away. It'll save me the bother of posting them.'

'They're lousy. Right? So you keep them. Do what you like with them.'

The sun had gone down below the roofs of the Co-op and the pub and the gloom was deepening.

'What do you want, then? Why did you come?'

A few moments passed before she answered. 'I don't know. See what you were like. I thought maybe you'd have something I needed. Like help. Right?'

'Help? What kind of help?'

'Forget it. I'd better be going.'

'How did you get here?'

'Taxi.'

'I'll drive you home.'

'No.

'Where do you live?'

'Near Henley. Can I ring from here?'

'Of course.'

I switched on the light and she looked in the telephone-directory, found a taxi service and dialled the number.

While we were waiting for the cab to fetch her I learned that she was married, aged thirty and had one child, a boy. She and her husband had led quite separate lives for the past five years, remaining under the same roof 'for the sake of the child' and for the more overtly selfish reasons of economic convenience. She wrote her telephone number on an empty envelope and put it

96

on my table. 'Call me if you like.'

'Is there any point?'

'There might be.' I was not sure whether or not there was a hint of invitation there.

'All right.'

After she had gone I felt restless and disinclined to go back to my Evelyn Waugh. She had been puzzling: annoying, attractive, shy, yet one sensed a strong undertow of arrogance. Her verbal style had irritated me, that upper middle-class voice aping some kind of trendy mid-Atlantic argot. I decided that she was probably a fool and a tiresome one, but I was not sure. Her scent was still in the room. Or perhaps I imagined it. Was she one of those literary camp-followers who, as Keats once said, 'would like to be married to a poem, and to be given away by a novel'? Somehow I doubted it. Certainly she had shown no visible respect. On the contrary her attitude, despite the superficial air of self-effacement, had been, if not patronizing, at least confident of her superiority. And that 'shyness' had been wholly self-regarding, a kind of *noli me tangere* that was based on a high estimate of the value of the goods and an assumption that they were pretty tempting to the touch. And so they were.

Sod her, I thought, and picked up the envelope on which she had written her telephone number, crumpled it up and threw it in the waste-paper basket. Soon the pub would be open and I would go for a drink.

The next morning I got up late. My only engagement for that day was a reading at Standlake School in the evening, so I had plenty of time to recover from the previous night's tippling with Jack and Brendan who had returned with me from the pub to the flat, each of us bearing bottles of various brews. My recollections of the later part of the session were indistinct. The living-room looked well-used. Cigarette-ends had been trodden into the carpet and the table-top was marked and stained. A score of bottles, some still containing drink, were scattered about the place and one chair was tipped onto its back. A cheerless sight. I decided to delay tidying it until I had drunk some coffee, bathed and shaved.

I picked up the mail from where it lay on the floor in the hall and went into the kitchen. While the water was boiling I swallowed a raw egg in Worcester Sauce and ate a cream cracker spread with butter and marmalade. Then I poured boiling water on my instant coffee, added sugar and dried milk, and settled at the kitchen table to read my mail. The only letter of real interest was from Lincoln Kirstein. He was, he wrote, coming to Britain on business and would be staying at the Connaught Hotel in London. He hoped that we would be able to meet. I checked the dates he had supplied against my diary and realized that he would be in England the following weekend. I would telephone him then and see what could be arranged.

It would be interesting to meet him, interesting and a little unnerving. Although, judging from the letters we had exchanged, we were much in accord over matters relating to poetry and we had both seen army service in the ranks during the war, I felt that there were probably large areas of activity which were of abiding fascination to him and of which I would be completely ignorant if not actively hostile to them. Ballet, for example, in which he was professionally involved and about which he had written a number of authoritative books, held little or no appeal for me. He was older than I by about a decade and a half and he was rich, expensively educated, sophisticated, with a wide circle of friends whose names were prominent in the Arts, and probably homosexual or bisexual. I would probably seem to him an uncouth lout, blundering and witless. Maybe I would be wiser to keep our relationship on an epistolary basis. But I knew that my curiosity would prevail and that I would not be able to resist the temptation to contact him that weekend.

I drank my coffee, bathed and shaved. Then I dressed and set myself to the task of cleaning up the living-room. I gathered up the glasses and bottles, poured any dregs down the kitchen sink, left the glasses ready for washing and hid the bottles away in the bottom of the store cupboard. Then I began to clear the table of ash-trays, conventional and improvised, cigarette-packets, stubs and other debris. While I was doing this I found the envelope on which Anna had written her telephone number. It had obviously been retrieved from the waste-paper basket and uncrumpled. I stared at it, trying to recall why I had reclaimed it from the rubbish. I could remember nothing about it. Perhaps I had telephoned her drunkenly, in the early hours of the morning. Perhaps? Almost certainly, for there could be no other reason for digging the envelope out and smoothing it so that the number was legible.

Very vaguely I remembered that Anna had not been entirely absent from my consciousness on the preceding evening. I did not think I had spoken of her to my companions, but she had been there, a diluted presence, teasing, a little irritating, but also desirable and elusive like a half-recalled melody or fragrance. There was only one thing to do and that was ring her up and see if I had disturbed her with my boozy maunderings. I could apologize, or attempt to. I sat down at the table and dialled the number on the envelope. I thought that perhaps this act might bring back the memory of having done it on the previous night but no recollection stirred. I heard the ringing at the other end of the line, the double rasp, one … two, one … two. I let it go on for quite a while and then hung up the receiver. She was not there. I felt slightly disappointed. Then I gave myself a shake and thought what the hell; she was a silly bitch, affected, probably neurotic, a tease. I would do well not to get involved. In any case she was young enough to be my daughter. I picked up the envelope, hesitated, then screwed it into a ball and again threw it away.

I spent the next weekend at Peter Porter's flat in Cleveland Square and on Monday morning went to the Connaught Hotel in Carlos Place where I had arranged to meet Lincoln Kirstein at eleven o'clock. The weather was pleasant, bright sunshine and a fresh breeze. I had enjoyed a restful couple of days with Peter and was feeling reasonably fit and clear-eyed. At the hotel Kirstein was informed by the hall porter of my arrival and it was not long before he appeared.

I cannot say that I was surprised by the way he looked, because I had formed no preconceived image of him, but I was certainly impressed. He was very tall, six feet two or three inches at least and his posture was upright, his movements assured. His head was so closely cropped that it was difficult to tell how much the bareness of his skull was due to baldness and how much to the exercise of clippers, but it was a fine head and it was held proudly with an imperious beak of a nose and shrewd, penetrating eyes. He was dressed soberly in a dark suit and a black, lightweight topcoat that was probably rainproof.

There was something that was at once ascetic and sensual about his features and the whole man exuded a sense of both physical and intellectual power and alertness.

We shook hands and he said how pleased he was at our meeting. Then he said, 'Would you like to take a walk? Or maybe we could take a boat to Greenwich.'

I said I would rather walk. We walked.

Oddly, I felt no awkward restraint and this fact was, I think, at least partly a consequence of his being American. His British counterpart – or the nearest possible approximation to it – would have paralyzed me with feelings of defensive and probably resentful inferiority. He would have been someone like the Director, say, of Covent Garden or Glyndebourne, a product of one of the most expensive public schools and Oxbridge, stylish, urbane, unsurprisable and effortlessly articulate. He would make me feel like the Hairy Ape or Tony Lumpkin. But Kirstein's good manners and style were of a different order. He was, or seemed to be, genuinely interested in anything I had to say. He asked questions and listened attentively to the answers. When he said that he was thrilled to be here in London with me after our exchange of letters he made it sound convincing. And he showed an unaffected zest for experience, a readiness to be impressed and to savour quite simple pleasures that a Britisher would almost certainly conceal, believing that these demonstrations would reveal immaturity and lack of sophistication. I think he was proud of his knowledge of London's geography and I was quite content for him to take the lead.

We walked quite a few miles that morning. Kirstein maintained a very lively pace for a man of seventy. He led me to Piccadilly, through Green Park and into St James's to the Guards' Chapel. Had I ever been inside? I had not, so he led the way into the building. Clearly it was not his first visit and there was something almost proprietory about the way in which he directed my attention to the features of the place that he thought were particularly beautiful or interesting. I found myself moved, despite the blatancy of the assault on the emotions. The silence was not merely the absence of noise; there was something positive in it, the quality of the suspended breath of awe.

The original chapel had been destroyed completely by a

flying-bomb near the end of the war. A service had been in progress and everyone in the place had been killed. A roll-call of the dead was inscribed on one wall and elsewhere were hung the colours of the various Guards Regiments, memorials of their battle-honours and the names of the great battlefields of the two World Wars: the Somme, Arras, Loos, Mons, Ypres, Tobruk, Alamein and Anzio, and there, too, was the still and soundless march of the killed in action. The rational man could shrug and smile at the absurdity of it all, the childishness, the drums and flags and bugles, all those toys that were meant to distract attention from the skeletal truth that war was brutal and obscene and the Church's evasions and casuistry contemptible. But the sense of tragedy, even of glory, somehow refused to accept dismissal and the heart was touched.

Over lunch Kirstein said, 'I was never in combat. I wish I had been. I guess I was near enough to know what it was like. But it's not the same thing.'

He had been on Paton's staff for a while and he told me that the fire-eating General was known to choose for his aides young men of equivocal sexual leanings who were often precious, elegant and sometimes downright effeminate. And he did this, not to provide for himself erotic distraction, but because he knew that such types were often recklessly brave and more willing to risk their lives than their ostensibly tougher and more masculine comrades. I mentioned Auden's poem on this theme, the one which ends:

> '... it is the pink-and-white,
> Fastidious, almost girlish, in the night
> When the proud-arsed broad-shouldered break and run,
> Who covers their retreat, dies at his gun.'

and the quotation led to discussion of the poet's work and, I suppose inevitably since Kirstein had known him well, his personality. I had met Auden only once, at the Edinburgh Festival in – if I remember correctly – 1964 and, partly because I held the man in such awe and partly because the encounter was very brief and formal, I carried away little impression of him except, of course, for that crumpled, face, the watchful, undeceivable eyes and the general effect of physical decrepitude out of all proportion to his chronological age. But I had heard from people who had been better acquainted with him that he had displayed traits of character that had been neither admirable nor endearing, a tendency to a spinsterish self-cosseting, greed, intolerance and a heartlessness that came close to cruelty. When I mentioned these judgements, rather hoping that Kirstein might contradict them, he nodded and with visible reluctance agreed that 'Wystan could be pretty tough at times.' Then he grinned ruefully: 'I'll give you an instance.'

Some years ago, when Auden was living in the United States, Kirstein suffered a severe mental breakdown.

'I went crazy,' he said.

'How crazy? What form did it take?'

'It was bad. I was violent. Dangerous. To other people and myself. I cut off my own toe. Yeah, I was crazy.'

He had been put into a mental hospital where he had remained for over a year before he was considered sufficiently well to return to the outside world. During the time of his incarceration Auden, who had been a close friend, did not visit him once, nor did he write or attempt to communicate in any way. When at last Kirstein was cured and was able to resume his former professional and social life he met up again with his old friend, the expatriate British poet, and he admitted to feeling some curiosity about the way Auden would behave after all those months of silence and neglect. The poet showed no embarrassment whatever and made only a single reference to Kirstein's illness and sojourn in hospital. He said, like a censorious Nanny, 'Don't do that again, Lincoln. It was very naughty of you.'

The anecdote was, in its way, quite funny but in view of the desperate seriousness of Kirstein's sickness it was also shocking. That Auden, as a young man, had been powerfully attracted to the theories of Homer Lane and Georg Groddeck, the founding fathers of psychosomatic medicine, was well known, so the view implied by his remark that Kirstein had chosen his illness was unsurprising; what was more revealing was the tone of the poet's reproof, the mixture of flippancy, disapproval and indifference to his friend's suffering, a tone that I found repugnant yet could not help believing was not uncharacteristic. Auden's poetry has given me at least as much pleasure as any other work of the last half-century and the admiration I hold for his skill, intelligence and versatility is

102

boundless, but I have felt, uneasily and for some years now, that those defects of personality revealed in Kirstein's story are debilitating presences in some – though by no means all – of his writings and might, in the eyes of posterity, relegate him from the very highest to a second place, albeit a brilliant one, in the order of the English poets of genius. In recounting the incident Kirstein showed no resentment at all and it was clear that his regard for his friend, which amounted almost to veneration, was undiminished.

We spoke of poetry, British and American, and he told me something of his experiences as an impresario of the ballet. His attitude to the dancers in his company was, I imagine, unusual for a balletomane for he regarded them not as artists but as acrobats; their skills were, he maintained, entirely physical and he felt that his involvement with the dance was a salutary escape from the cerebral and sedentary life into a world that was closer to that of the athlete than the artist. But wherever our conversation wandered it continually returned to the subject of war and the military life. The reason for this was partly because we had first made contact with each other through his war poems and their use in my book on the poetry of World War II and partly because of a similarity, despite the obvious differences, in temperament and age. We parted with promises to keep in touch and I picked up my van from the car park at Paddington Station and drove back to Berinsfield.

The visit to the Guards' Chapel and our exchanges of wartime reminiscences directed my thoughts insistently back to my days in the army, not so much to memories of battle but to the grinding tedium of service in the United Kingdom, training, manoeuvres, guards, courses, discomfort, humiliation, frustration, boredom and – rarely but unforgettably – moments of bizarre comedy, excitement and the joy of extraordinary physical well-being when food, warmth and rest were not commonplace elements which we had the automatic right to expect in the pattern of our days but pleasures of real intensity, positive blessings. I do not believe that I have ever idealized or romanticized the experience of army service; I knew quite well that I was often wretchedly miserable and almost always less than content, but there was something weirdly seductive about occupying the lowest rank, about the minimal expectations you encountered in your superiors, the reduction of your demands on life to the primitive. When I rebelled it was usually with the result that I became embedded more deeply in the mire of primitive existence, that is to say that I would end up in the guard-room where the last vestiges of dignity or humanity, if such still survived, were ripped away.

I think it was the second privilege leave I was granted after serving for almost a year that I failed to return to my unit in the North of Scotland. It happened like this. I had no intention of going absent-without-leave. I had spent my leave in London, staying at the Union Jack Club near Waterloo Station, and I was packed and ready to go back in plenty of time. In those early days of the war we had to carry all of our equipment with us when we went on leave: large pack and small pack, webbing, ammunition pouches, rifle, bayonet, water-bottle, gas-cape, ground-sheet, respirator, steel helmet strapped to the large valise and kit-bag, that huge canvas sausage containing spare battledress, boots, underwear, shirts and so on. I lugged this lot to King's Cross Station to catch the 7.35 to Inverness.

I arrived a good three-quarters of an hour before the train was due to leave and, as soon as it pulled into the station. I found a compartment and reserved myself a seat by dumping the kit-bag on the luggage-rack and placing the rest of my stuff, including the rifle, next to the window. When that was done I left the carriage and walked along the platform to the barrier. I showed the ticket-collector my travel-warrant and said, 'I'm just going for a drink. I've left my kit on the train.'

'Leaves at 7.35. Don't go and miss it, chum.'

'I won't.'

I found the buffet which was crowded, mainly by members of the Forces, most of whom seemed to be at the bar struggling to get served. I joined the crowd, pushing and shouldering my way through. A sailor just in front of me squeezed through to a place at the counter and, as he glanced triumphantly over his shoulder, he probably saw the look of frustration or desperation on my face and took pity on me, for he said, 'I'll get yours, Jock. What is it?' I told him a pint of bitter.

'I'll double-bank,' he said. 'It's the only way.'

Five minutes later we struggled clear of the worst of the crowd, each of us clutching two pints of beer.

I said, 'How much do I owe you?'

'Skip it. I'm loaded. No kidding. Cheers.'

I felt grateful but rather embarrassed by his generosity. We drank quickly.

I said, 'You fancy a short? Scotch, rum or something?'

'I told you. I'm loaded. I wouldn't say so if I wasn't. My brother's got a caff in Stepney, his own business. Lucky bastard's failed his medical. Every time I come ashore he tries to bury me in pound-notes. Guilt, see? Feels guilty 'cause he's a civvy. Suits me – Hey! There's a space at the bar. Be back in a tick.'

The sailor went to the bar and came back with two more pints and two whiskies.

'Where you stationed?' he asked.

'Fort George.'

'Christ! I was up that way last year. Bloody awful it was.'

'Where are you heading for?'

'Greenock; going to join a mine-sweeper.'

'You catching the 7.35?'

He was.

I said, 'We've time for one more if we make it a quick one ... No, no, you've bought more than enough. I'm getting them. Hang on.'

I attacked the bar again and, after some shouting and gesticulating, I managed to get two more whiskies. I returned to where my sailor friend and I had been standing to find that he was no longer there. Maybe he had gone to the lavatory. I drank one of the whiskies. The clock above the bar showed that it was almost seven-thirty. Where the hell had he got to? I peered around but could see no sign of him. Well, I could wait no longer. I knocked back the other drink and made for the door but, as I did so, there was a sudden insurge of new customers and it took me some time to resist being carried back into the centre of the buffet and fight my way through on to the platform. I reached the barrier in time to see the train, carrying all of my kit, gathering speed as it left the station.

My first reaction was one of incredulous horror but this was succeeded very quickly and a little surprisingly by a feeling that was remarkably close to exhilaration. There was not another train until the next day and there was nothing I could do to avoid being at least twenty-four hours late and this would mean an automatic charge of being AWOL. The loss of all my military possessions, including rifle and ammunition, would not increase my popularity with my superiors. What the hell; I might as well be hanged for a sheep. So I stayed in London for three days, after which I was stopped by a military policeman, asked for my pass, taken into custody and held until an escort from my unit could take me back to face retribution.

By the time I was brought before the Commanding Officer for trial my kit had been found and returned to the Fort though my carelessness in losing it did nothing to help my cause. I was sentenced to twenty-one days' Field Punishment to be served in the Regimental Guard-room. Those three weeks were uncomfortable but nowhere near unbearable and I thought the price for three days' extra leave well worth paying. I had suffered the lesser punishments for petty offences, Confined to Barracks, fatigues and so on, but my stay in the Guard-room was my initiation into the army's underworld and it had a curiously liberating effect. From then on there was no question of my conforming, of making the least effort to be a 'good soldier', of considering for a moment the prospect of promotion. I had reached the lowest stratum of military life where such notions as decency, truthfulness, industry, patriotism and dignity were either totally meaningless or the comical delusions of the over-privileged. Once you had become a 'detention-wallah' you could be reduced no further; you could not be insulted or shamed. You had found something like the freedom of the baby or lunatic; the danger lay in the likelihood of being trapped there forever.

I thought that it was interesting that since I had come to Berinsfield I had found myself thinking about the more anarchic and disreputable moments in my youth, times of poverty, violence and aggressive non-conformity, as if the relative solitariness and sense of displacement of the present was moving in parallel to related events of the past and was revivifying them in the memory. Not that my life in Berinsfield was anything like as grim as my army days had been, but it shared something of their quality: my companions were mainly masculine and their values were very similar to those held in the barrack-room, crude concepts of loyalty and friendship, gross materialism and sentimentality, coarse and brutal humour. And I felt, too, that the main direction of my life had been arrested for the period of my stay; like army service the Fellowship was an interruption, not necessarily fruitless but essentially irrelevant, something to live through and, if possible, profit from, before returning to the main route.

106

The evening after my meeting with Lincoln Kirstein I was in The Berinsfield Arms with Brendan and Jack when a stranger came into the bar. It was obvious that he was fairly drunk though not, it seemed, troublesomely so, and the barman showed no hesitation in serving him. He was drinking neat whiskies chased by half-pints of bitter and, if this were not enough to establish his nationality, his accent removed any lingering doubt. He spoke with the rising cadence that falls away at the end of each phrase that is peculiar to Glasgow and the voice had the throaty hoarseness of the Gorbals hard-case. I had met many such during my time in the Gordon Highlanders – fly-men, hard nuts, who would 'put the heid on you' as soon as look at you, loyal and wildly generous friends, but formidable enemies.

This man was built to pattern, short, compact with fairly wide shoulders for his height, and a head which looked small and neat on the strong neck. His eyes were dark, deeply set under heavy brows, and his chin was prominent and aggressive. Even when he was standing still he seemed to be strutting. He had taken a place next to me at the bar and I could feel his ill-focused interest settling on me and my companions.

I was not surprised nor especially pleased when he said, 'What you having, Jimmy? You and your friends. Come now. Drink up and have a wee yin on me.'

I said, 'We've just filled up, thanks. We're okay for now.'

He spoke to the barman: 'Fill 'em up. Give 'em what they want. I'll have the same again. Go on, never mind what they say. Give 'em all a drop o' whisky.'

The barman put whisky in front of us. Brendan wore an expression that managed to mix slightly amused tolerance with reserve and even a touch of that disapproval which is commonly found in the habitual drinker who, when sober, encounters someone patently under the influence. But he raised his glass and said, without warmth, 'Cheers.'

Jack, always more companionable and never censorious, said, 'All the best. Haven't seen you in here before.'

The Scotsman ignored him but looked at me with a gaze that caricatured shrewd appraisal and was accompanied by a small knowing smirk. 'Hey you,' he said, 'where've I seen you before?'

I raised my drink and said, 'Cheers.'

'Come on, now. I've seen you some place before. What d'ye

107

do? What's your job?'

'Not much,' I said. 'Have a drink.'

He was not to be distracted. 'I know you from somewhere. What d'you do for a living?'

Jack said, 'He's a poet.'

The Scotsman still took no notice of him. 'What's wrong with you? Why d'you no want to tell me what you do for a living? Ashamed, are you? Is that the size of it? Come on. What work d'ye do?'

I said, rather uncomfortably, 'I'm a writer.'

'A waiter?'

'No. A writer.'

'Writer? What d'ye mean, you're a writer? What's your business? What kind o' work d'ye do?'

'He's told you,' Jack said. 'He's a writer.'

'I'm no talking to you, Jimmy. I'm asking him. Come on. Tell us. What's your work? I'll tell you what I am. I'm a contractor. I employ twenty men. That's what I do. Now you tell me what you do.'

I was getting bored by this. I said slowly and carefully, 'I've told you and my friend's told you. I'm a writer, an author, I write books and other things. That's my job. That's what I do for a living. Okay?'

He stared at me with his cunning, knowledgeable smirk. Then he gave a little shrug and turned back to his drink. I began to talk to Brendan about Mel's forthcoming fight that had been arranged to take place in Luton.

'Hey, Jimmy! Listen!'

I had half turned away from the Glaswegian. I looked over my shoulder at him.

'What I want to know is where I've seen you before,' he said. Then he added, 'Where d'ye work?'

Jack laughed and Brendan looked disgusted.

I said. 'Look. I've told you what I do for a living. If you can't understand, that's too bad. I can't put it any simpler. So let's drop it, shall we?' I turned back to resume my chat with Brendan.

'Hey, you! Don't you turn your back on me, Jimmy.' I felt a light jab on the right shoulder-blade.

I faced him again. 'Okay. You bought us a drink. Very kind of you. Drink that up and I'll get you one. But it doesn't mean you've bought our attention for the whole evening. I told you in the first place we didn't want a drink. You insisted on buying. That's your look-out. I don't want to be rude or unfriendly or anything. You asked me a question and I gave you the answer. About half-a-dozen times. I don't think we've ever met before. I've told you what I do for a living. I'll tell you once more. I'm a writer. I work for myself. I'm free-lance. I don't do any other job. That clear? You understand?'

'Writing,' he said with incredulous contempt, 'that's no work!'

Surprisingly it was Brendan who answered. 'What d'you mean writing's not work? How much writing you ever done? How many books you ever wrote? You think a man's got to be swinging a pick before you can say he's working. Any fool can swing a pick or dig a ditch. It's not everybody can write books and poetry.'

The Scot was beyond reasoning but this did not prevent him from arguing. But his belligerence, which had never been far from the surface, was reduced now and what was left of it was entirely verbal. I think that he sensed in Brendan someone who would be actively provoked rather than intimidated by threats of physical violence and, if it came to a show-down, the Irishman might well emerge victorious. When I left them to it he had adopted an almost ingratiating tone and was moving into the maudlin stage.

I said goodnight and went back to the flat and, after a supper of biscuits and cheese and a mug of coffee, I undressed and got into bed. I read a bit of 'The Dunciad' but my eyes were smarting from the smoke in the pub and concentration was slipping so I switched off the light and settled down to sleep. As I lay there I thought of the Glaswegian and Brendan's defence of my vocation as 'work' which had been so unexpected and rather touching since he had previously seemed to view the art of poetry as something slightly comical and perhaps not quite decent. Yet he had affirmed its composition as hard work with more confidence than I would have been able to muster had the apologetics been left to me.

Writing, poetry or prose, was of course work, but I felt that it was closer to strenuous play than to the labours of the farmer, baker, carpenter, engineer or truck-driver whose efforts were justified by their providing a necessary commodity or service

109

without which the social order would be disrupted. I knew the arguments used to defend the poet's rôle in society, the proposition that he was the custodian of language, that he 'purified the dialect of the tribe' or that he acted as its conscience and enriched the quality of life, and I supposed that I believed these things. Yet I found it very easy to sympathize with the Scotsman's attitude and that of millions like him who had never voluntarily read a poem in their lives and had never felt the slightest wish to do so.

Perhaps it was the puritanical work-ethic that had been instilled into me by my upbringing that caused feelings of guilt at being able to live by writing. Or perhaps it was an uncertainty about the quality of my work. It was all very well to speak of rescuing the language from its cynical misuse by politicians and journalists and of the poet's contribution to the cultural heritage of man, and when one thought of the work of Shakespeare, Milton, Wordsworth, Hardy and Yeats, unqualified assent was the only response possible; but not all the people who had written or were now writing what they claimed was poetry were so gifted, indeed many seemed without any talent at all, and how could I be sure I was not among them? I knew, or had known, personally many men and women who lacked the most elementary qualifications as writers, who were stupid, vain, and ignorant of the rudimentary principles of the craft they claimed to practise, yet they were far more vociferous in their claims to be supported by the State and honoured by the public as artists than infinitely more accomplished writers, many of whom followed other and demanding professions in order to earn money and time for the exercise of their literary gifts, and the thought of being numbered among those absurd pretenders was not one to induce comfortable sleep. Yet perhaps there was a modest but honourable place in the order of things for people like me for, to survive at all, a literary culture must have its honest minor authors, the other-ranks in the army of the immortals. Maybe. But I was by then so tired that I could worry about the matter no more. I slept and dreamed that I was in prison.

SIX

THE NEXT DAY WAS, as I see from my diary, Thursday, April the first, All Fool's Day and, shortly after eleven o'clock in the morning, as I was working or trying to work at the umpteenth draft of a poem called 'Old Man in Winter', the telephone rang. I cursed and picked up the instrument. The voice at the other end of the line was a woman's and it was familiar yet elusive. I felt that I knew it well, or had known it well, perhaps in the far past, but maddeningly I could not identify it now. Of course it would have been difficult to recognize, however well-known, for the woman spoke only one word, 'Hello.'

I waited and then said, 'Who is it?'

There was another interval of silence before she spoke again. 'Don't you know?'

This was not the kind of game I much enjoyed playing at any time, far less since I wanted to get back to my poem.

I said, 'Who's speaking?'

'Haven't you any idea?'

'Yes.'

'You have? Who is it then?'

'Mabel.'

'Who?'

'Auntie Mabel. I'd know your voice anywhere.' I hung up.

Half a minute later the ringing started again. I picked up the receiver and waited.

She said, 'All right. I'm sorry. It's me. Anna.'

I felt a quick spurt of pleasure, a small excitement which was at once followed by a faint uneasiness, a vague sense of being threatened.

I said, 'How are you?'

She gave an odd grunt of laughter but did not say anything.

After the silence had persisted for a few seconds I asked her if she wanted to speak to me for any particular reason.

She said, 'Do you remember ringing me up the other night?'

'The other ... Oh ... yes ... well, er, not very clearly.'

'No.'

'No, I'm afraid I don't remember at all clearly.'

'You mean you don't remember at all.'

'Only very vaguely.'

111

'You don't remember anything do you?'

'No.'

She laughed again, briefly, angrily perhaps. 'I didn't think you would.'

'What did I say?'

'Not much that made any sense. You wanted to see me. Or so you said. Repeatedly.'

'I'm sorry. It must have been boring.'

'Not exactly.'

There was more silence. The telephone was a cup of darkness. I thought I could hear her breathing. Then she said, 'Do you want to see me now? I don't mean now immediately. I mean now you're sober.'

Did I? The instant response was affirmative yet, even as assent was recognized, qualifications came flooding in to prevent its being voiced. I was too old. She had said so herself. I did not want the distractions of an affair. It was difficult enough already to get any work done. The excitement, fever, fret, jealousy, doubt, longing, the certainty that this could not be a casual, uncomplicated thing, it would all become obsessive, no time and energy would be left over for anything else. I had been through it all too often. I knew I no longer possessed the stamina. I knew the thing would be doomed from the start. I was too old, shagged out. After a while, a year at the most, maybe a few months or even weeks, she would be attracted by someone of her own age and I would be given the brush-off, rejected, humiliated, a bad sad joke. I could do well without any of it.

'Yes,' I said.

'When?'

'Any time. What about this evening?'

A pause. Then she said a little doubtfully, 'I might be able to get out for an hour or so. That's all. Could you come over here? There's a pub called The Lamb. We could meet there. It's on the main road from Dorchester. You couldn't miss it. It's a creepy place. Oak beams and pewter tankards. Aston Martins in the car park. You know?'

'What time will you be there?'

'I don't know. I've got to fix a sitter. About eight. I ought to manage it by eight.'

'Okay. I look forward to it.'

She repeated the name of the pub and we rang off.

That evening I allowed myself plenty of time to find the place and arrived shortly after half-past seven. Anna was right about the creepiness of the pub. It was full of horse-brasses, sporting prints and people with loud voices rich with self-confidence and stupidity. The landlord made a great show of calling me 'sir' in his Eton and Brigade of Guards accent but his pale little eyes were disdainful as they noted the shabbiness of my clothes. I carried my pint of bitter to a table as far from the bar as I could get and took from my pocket the paperback selection of Browning's poems that I had prudently brought with me and began to read. At eight o'clock I had my glass refilled, lit a cigarette and returned to Browning, but now I found it difficult to fix my attention on the page and I repeatedly glanced up from the book to the entrance to the bar. Three young men came in and began to talk in penetrating tones about their cars. I put my paperback away and drank some beer. I would give her another ten minutes, then leave.

At twenty past eight my second pint was almost finished. I got out the book again and decided to read 'A Toccata of Galuppi's', a poem I knew so well that it would make little demand on my power to concentrate, and, if she had not arrived by the time I had finished reading the work, I would clear off. I had reached the last line of the penultimate stanza – 'What of soul was left, I wonder, when the kissing had to stop?' – when I sensed her presence close to the table. She was looking down at me, smiling, and I saw that she had one arm in a plaster cast supported by a sling. She sat down.

I said, 'You're half an hour late.'

'I know. I couldn't get away. Baby-sitter was late.' She offered no apology.

'What do you want to drink?'

'Vodka.'

'You want anything in it? Tonic? Lime?'

'All right.'

'Which?'

'What?' She looked vaguely puzzled.

'Which do you want? Tonic or Lime?'

'Oh, either. Tonic.'

I went to the bar and returned with the drinks.

'What have you done to your arm?'

113

'I think it's more a question of what *you* did to it.'

I was not sure that I had heard her correctly. Certainly I had not understood. 'Me? What are you talking about?'

'Well, it wouldn't have happened except for you.'

'Oh?' When she did not elaborate I said, 'What do you mean? How could I have hurt your arm?'

Conversation with her seemed to be like a game, the rules and even the goal of which one had almost no knowledge.

She said, 'I fell downstairs.'

'And how am I to blame for that?'

'I was coming down to answer the phone.'

'Oh.' I was beginning to see what she was getting at. 'That was when I rang you.'

'Yes.'

'Well, I'm very sorry you hurt yourself but I can't say I feel responsible. It was an accident.'

'If you hadn't phoned it wouldn't have happened, right?'

'If there hadn't been any stairs it wouldn't have happened either. If you want to be safe you'd better live in a bungalow and get yourself cut off the phone.' Then I added, 'Right?'

She grinned faintly and took a drink of her vodka. Then she said, 'Of course I don't really blame you. Not now. I did though at the time. And how I did. I know you'll think that's irrational but try and see it from my end. The phone rings at about one in the morning. I was fast asleep. I got up more than half asleep still. Staggered half way down the stairs and then went arse over tip. It hurt! It bloody well hurt! And then, when I'd finished moaning and swearing what do I find? A slobbering drunk at the other end of the line. I was not pleased.'

'I can imagine.'

Anna said, 'Get me another drink.'

'Please...' I suggested, like a gently admonitory parent with a wilful child.

Her head went slightly to one side she looked at me speculatively. 'You're very unsure of yourself, aren't you? Like insecure?'

'Why? Because I don't like being given orders?'

'Something like that.'

I pushed back my chair and reached for her glass.

'No,' she said. 'I don't really want one. Anyway, I don't like this place. Let's split.'

114

I finished my beer and we went out into the car park and got into my van.

I said, 'Where do you want to go?'

She shrugged.

I felt suddenly sick of the situation, sick of her, of myself, and guilty because I knew she wanted some kind of help from me and I was too lazy, selfish and lacking in sympathy even to try to discover the nature of her need, far less attempt to supply whatever it was she needed. The plaster cast on her arm accused me. She was hurt and her first accusation had been true. I was responsible.

We sat in the stationary van, saying nothing. The sky was slowly darkening.

I said, 'I'll take you home.'

'No. I'll walk. It's not far. I'd rather.'

She waited a few moments, perhaps for me to protest, to insist on driving her. Then, without looking at me, she got out of the van and slammed the door. I sat and watched her walk away. She moved with extraordinary grace. The ankle-length skirt she wore made her look very tall; it lent her an old-fashioned aspect like that of a Victorian romantic heroine, one of those beautiful sacrificial victims of men and destiny from a Hardy novel. Yet there was something childlike there, too, something forlorn and lost. Or maybe I was sentimentalizing the whole dreary thing. I smoked a cigarette and then drove back to Berinsfield.

I slept badly that night, teased and nibbled at by vague uneasiness, desire, regret. I could not dismiss the vision of Anna, especially her eyes, their wariness, vulnerability, the dark, opalescent mystery. Things about her which had irritated me now seemed piquant, her adoption of mid-Atlantic locutions spoken with the accent of the middle-class Home Counties, her conscious efforts at charmlessness. I was tempted to telephone her – and probably break her other arm, I told myself sourly. There were moments when I felt an acute sense of loss, the heart-sickening knowledge of having wantonly turned away from something precious that was within my grasp and would never be so again. And then I would be become aware of a sly and opposing current of feeling that insisted on being recognized as that of relief. I wanted Anna, but stronger than the desire was the fear of the consequences, the fear of the pain of ultimate rejection, of contempt and ridicule. Sleep finally came but it was populous with shapes of disquiet.

That week my book on poetry of the Second World War, *Not Without Glory,* was published and the event helped greatly to keep thoughts of Anna at a more comfortable distance for I was busy with radio and press interviews and diverted by a party given by my publishers at The National Book League headquarters in Albemarle Street. The party was a pleasant occasion and I enjoyed drinking with old friends, many of whom I had not seen for some time. Dannie Abse and Dennis Enright both seemed in excellent health and spirits, and Roy Fuller looked enviably young and more like a retired army officer or a pre-war colonial administrator than one of our best living poets; Elizabeth Thomas, who was at that time on *The New Statesman,* was her usual sympathetic and entirely engaging self. It was good, too, to see Jean and John Burney, down from Yorkshire, an old drinking partner and gifted amateur of poetry, Ron Reeves and, perhaps the most unexpected and pleasurable surprise, Jean Stead, whom I had first met almost thirty years before in Leeds, when she was a cub reporter on *The Yorkshire Post,* and who was now the news editor of *The Guardian.* Whether the party repaid the time and money invested in it by my publishers is, I would guess, rather unlikely, but it was for me a memorable evening.

I spent a couple of nights in London and drove back to Berinsfield in time to give an evening reading and talk to the Dorchester-on-Thames Arts Society. Back from the rather hectic pleasures of the capital and suffering slightly from too much wine and too little sleep I had small appetite for the proceedings but my host and the audience, all middle-class and at least middle-aged, were courteous and generally amiable and I think the meeting was considered a success. The questions and discussion which followed my reading came to an end at about nine-thirty and, as I was preparing to leave, a lady in unmagical grey tweed and hair approached and asked me if I had far to travel. Only a couple of miles, I told her, just along the road, to Berinsfield.

Her mouth opened and her eyes grew wider. 'Berinsfield! Surely you don't live there!' There was no mistaking the dismay. Evidently she had not heard that I was the Resident Poet there. I explained how I had been sent there by the Southern Arts Association.

'Oh, you poor man, what a ghastly place to send you!'

She could not have sounded more appalled if I had told her that I had been appointed court jester to President Amin.

I said, 'Do you know the place?'

She shuddered. 'I've not actually been there but I know all about it. Dreadful things one hears. Quite uncivilized. Violence. Women with no...oh dear, all kinds of frightful things.' A man came up and said to me, 'Would you care for a glass of sherry before you go?'

The woman said, 'Edward, this poor man lives in Berinsfield.'

'Yes, dear, I know. Medium or dry?'

'No sherry thanks. I've really got to be on my way.'

I said my goodbyes and went out to the van. I was quite surprised to find that I had felt an annoyed defensiveness about Berinsfield. All right, it was a dump, but there were things about it that I found more appealing than the Thames Valley thatched and timbered villages that looked like sets for dull second feature British movies. If I hurried back to the community centre I would have time for a couple of pints before they put up the shutters in the club.

Jack and Brendan were in the bar and I was pleased to see them.

'You've not been around for a few days,' Jack said.

'I was in London.'

Brendan looked shrewd, smiled and nodded to himself. He knew all about London, the birds and the booze.

Jack asked, 'Business or pleasure?'

'Business really. Or a bit of both.' I told him about the book, the publication party, the radio broadcasts on 'Kaleidoscope' and a programme called 'Jack de Manio Precisely'.

'Great publicity,' Jack said. 'That'll help to sell the book.'

I doubted it.

Brendan said, 'What's your man like then? This de Manio?'

'He's all right.' The fact was I had found the broadcaster rather boring and, while I could not blame him for his total ignorance of and lack of interest in poetry, I though he could have attempted to modify his tone of fruity and complacent philistinism for the few minutes of our conversation.

'Is he Eyetalian or something? That's never an English name, de Manio.'

'He looks and sounds English enough.'

Brendan shook his head slowly, unconvinced.

At the shout of last orders we had a final round of drinks and left the club. We exchanged goodnights and each of us departed for his own home.

I slept soundly that night and the next day, which was free of any commitments, I went into Oxford, had lunch in a pub and then visited Blackwell's bookshop in the Broad. There I found that a surprisingly large stack of my *Not Without Glory* was on sale but I detected no eagerness on the part of customers to buy. I was quite pleased at the book's prominence among those recently published but the pleasure I felt was mild and I reflected that the old excitement of bringing out a new work had been toned down by time and disappointments to a tremor so mild that it was scarcely perceptible. Still, I thought, I might as well buy myself a commemorative gift. My publishers now owed me the second advance, due on date of publication, not a very large sum but enough to justify a little self-indulgence. So I bought the paperback edition of *The Selected Letters of James Joyce,* edited by Richard Ellman, and Sylvia Plath's *Letters Home,* both of which had recently received a good deal of attention in the literary press. Then, after an aimless walk, made sadly enjoyable by the fine spring weather and the many beautiful girls who floated through the sunlight, I made my way to the car park, climbed into the van and drove back to Berinsfield.

The next day the first review of *Not Without Glory* appeared in *The Daily Telegraph.* It was written by the poet, Elizabeth Jennings, and while – understandably enough – it did not attempt anything in the way of deep criticism, it was well-informed and decidedly approving in tone. This was probably the very best I could expect and I felt that my publishers should be well pleased. The next weekend I got up latish on Sunday morning, bathed and shaved and went to fetch the newspapers before going to The Berinsfield Arms for my usual Sunday lunch-time drink. In the pub I settled in a quiet corner, relieved to see that there was no one in the bar likely to interrupt my lonely pleasures, and I opened *The Observer* at the book pages.

Immediately I saw that my book was reviewed, and at considerable length, by Kingsley Amis. I read the article with some bewilderment and not a little annoyance. To my surprise Amis had treated what I thought of as a fairly simple survey of Second World War poetry in the English language as some kind of personal testment, a statement of my attitudes, not to poetry, but to the war, to military life and to politics. In his first paragraph he wrote of the Second World War:

> 'Over thirty years after the event, when most of his contempararies look back with sentimental affection or at least with tolerance, he [i.e. Scannell] is still smarting at the humiliation of being reshaped by the military machine, the mindlessness of the soldier's life, the isolation, the anxiety, the enslavement, the boredom – especially that.'

Certainly these things were a large part of life as I knew it as a soldier but whether or not I was still smarting from those old injuries and insults thirty years later is beside the point. What I was trying to make clear in the book was that much of the best poetry of World War II was concerned with precisely these threats to the wholeness and dignity of being human – Henry Reed's 'Lessons of the War' is an obvious example – and that these preoccupations produced, formal considerations aside, a different kind of poetry from that written in the 1914-18 war. As for my failure to look back with sentimental affection to the war, I would have to plead guilty to the charge, though I very much doubted whether as many of my contemporaries as Amis claimed felt so tenderly towards their days in uniform.

Over the next week or two other reviews appeared. John Lehman was sympathetic in *The Sunday Telegraph* and Jon Silkin wrote a conscientious and thoughtful piece in *New Society*. Then came the one that staggered me. In *The New Statesman* of May 28th 1976 John Carey reviewed my book under the heading *Futility*, a title which was not calculated to reassure. That anyone should disagree with my judgements of individual poems or poets or find fault with my style or with the way my material was organized was something to be expected. What I did not expect was the note of personal venom, of contemptuous loathing that my unambitious little essay aroused in Professor

119

Carey. His contribution to *The New Statesman* was less a review than an explosion of bile, and his rage, as extreme passion is apt to do, so affected his reason that he lashed out with extraordinary charges. For example, he took me to task for failing to mention 'Desmond Graham's fine biography of Douglas' (i.e. the poet Keith Douglas who was killed in Normandy in 1944) which book, he added, 'might have been noticed, you'd think, by even casual perusers of literary columns.' In fact I had reviewed the biography myself in the literary columns of the very journal in which the learned professor was sounding off and the reason why I had not mentioned it in my book was very simple: I had not heard of it, which was not surprising since it had not been published at the time of *Not Without Glory*'s going to press.

Carey took strong exception to my lack of admiration for Rupert Brooke's sonnet, 'If I should die…'and he told his readers that this was 'a poem that must have brought comfort to thousands, and, one might add, may have the edge in that respect on the Collected Works of Vernon Scannell.' Quite apart from the childish jeering at the non-existent 'Collected Works of Vernon Scannell', it did strike me as curious that an Oxford Professor of Literature, who no doubt prided himself on his rigorous critical standards and method, should so passionately defend a poem on the sole ground that it 'must have brought comfort to thousands'. It hardly needs pointing out that, by Carey's criterion, two of our most estimable living poets must be Patience Strong and Pam Ayres.

My immediate reaction to reading the piece was to search my memory for any recollection of having encountered the man, for such outrage, I felt, could only be caused by my having offended him personally or caused him some kind of injury. I looked again at the review, searching for some clue to its author's fury but could find none, just the insulting words and phrases, tumbling over one another in their frenzy to get onto the page. I was 'dogmatic', my 'critical sympathy minuscule'; I showed 'mechanical obtuseness', my 'insensitivity almost always outdoes expectation', and so on. At one point he misquoted some general remarks I had made contrasting the attitudes and beliefs of the generation of servicemen in the 1939-45 War with those of their fathers in the Great War and he triumphantly demanded to be told how I could possibly know whether these

120

feelings were common to all of the armed forces in World War II since my own experience, he shrewdly pointed out, 'was limited to the Gordon Highlanders'. Could he possibly think that, because I had served with one particular regiment, I could have no knowledge of how soldiers in other units felt? Or, for that matter, of the feelings of people serving in other branches of the armed services?

I know nothing of Carey's writings other than occasional journalism nor, indeed, whether he has written anything of note. Paul Fussell was a different case. I knew that he, like Carey, was an academic, but I knew more of him than that. I had quite recently read one of his books, *The Great War and Modern Memory,* and had been deeply impressed by its intelligence, insight, the liveliness of its prose and its lack of pedantry. So when I saw that he was reviewing *Not Without Glory* in *The Times Literary Supplement* of 11th July I felt real apprehension. If he were to take the same line as Carey had done then I would have to face the fact that in my amateurish venture into the field of academic criticism I revealed not mere ineptitude but offensive ignorance, stupidity and lack of taste. A glance showed me that Fussell's review was dauntingly long. If this were to be an attack on the Carey scale I would be annihilated. I began to read with trepidation which quickly turned to relief and then to grateful pleasure when I saw that every one of Carey's condemnations was reversed and that the whole review was a sympathetic discussion of all the points I had tried to make in my book.

But I have been digressing and moving ahead of events in Berinsfield at that time, the end of April. With the approaching summer I found myself more content and more sure than I had hitherto been that I was not, after all, entirely parasitical on the community. I gave another reading to the children at the Abbey Junior School in Berinsfield and again found my young audience unaffectedly enthusiastic. After the session one of the English teachers rather shyly confessed that she wrote short stories and asked me if I would have a look at some of her work. The stories turned out to be better than most of those which one sees from unpublished writers and I was pleased to find that the weaknesses were of the order that can be easily and inoffensively discussed and rectified; in other words the flaws were not those of sensibility, failure in imagination and tact, that could not be mentioned without implied criticism of the author's personality, but structural and textual misjudgements that could be objectively focused upon and about which practical suggestions for improvement could be made. I was managing also at this time to do a little work of my own and I found the flat less oppressive. Not even Berinsfield could be entirely unlovely in the newly cleansed shimmer of the spring sunlight. On the whole, I thought, things were going pretty well, and the next three months ought to be increasingly pleasant and productive.

I often thought of Anna but made no attempt to communicate with her. Once or twice, usually late at night after drinking in the pub or club, I would feel lonely, self-pitying and randy in the blurred, sentimental way of the middle-aged and half-sloshed, and I would play my cassettes of the Elgar Cello Concerto or the Mozart Clarinet Quintet, which I was finding especially addictive at that time, and I would reach out for the telephone. But either I would not lift it from its cradle or, if I got so far, I would replace it without dialling. I now believe that a deep instinct for not only self-preservation, but the preservation of possibility, prevented me and would go on preventing me from ever re-establishing contact with Anna. She was someone I could keep. The situation – if such a fortuitous and inconsequential cluster of incidents could be given that name – was something that should never be resolved. I could keep it, sentimentally, self-deceivingly, to savour in the future with its appropriate weather, music and images, my lost encounter, brief weekend, an ersatz regret, an inextinguishable perhaps. So I did not telephone, then or ever, and I did not see Anna again.

SEVEN

In MAY THE LONG HOT SUMMER had already begun. The mornings were eager with the sense of undisclosed promise, the sunlight reached into the dusty corners of the flat and, out of doors, it leaped flashing from windscreens of cars, glittering on the chrome; its exuberance was echoed in the voices of the street; people called greetings to each other, speech grew close to song, there was laughter, all was unclenched and warm now, after the dark months stretched under cold and sackcloth skies. Girls wore summer dresses, their legs and shoulders white and startled in the dazzle. The 'Green', on which the little modern church had been built, was, for the first time since I had known it, truly green. It was here, at weekends and in the evenings, after working-hours, that the male youth of Berinsfield gathered to pass the time in argument and horseplay, punctuated by frequent and loud guffaws, and in crude collective courtship of such girls as happened to walk by, an activity, I suspected, that was an end in itself, hopeless and onanistic. A few of the boys owned motor-cycles and in their spacemen's helmets and black leather jackets, which looked as if they had been hammered on to the backs of the riders with large silver-headed nails, they made ear-drilling circuits of the Green or sat astride their stationary machines in postures of proud and masculine dominance.

John Wright ran a youth club where table-tennis and similar games could be played but these facilities were used mainly by younger children and, once the boys started work, they regarded the club as a part of their outgrown childhood. The average age of the youngsters who haunted the Green was about seventeen. Sometimes they would obtain bottles or cans of beer from the pub's off-sales department and then the shouting and the laughter would become more raucous, sometimes moving out of control towards the edge of hysteria, but they seemed a harmless, slightly pitiable group, stranded uneasily between childhood and manhood, bored, restless, ill-equipped to utilize or enjoy their leisure, bewildered and frustrated.

God knew what they did or where they did it in the winter months. Perhaps they stayed at home watching television or maybe they visited each other's homes. Whatever it was they did it was obvious that summer was the time for their emergence into the light. In the evenings, when I crossed the road to The Berinsfield Arms, they would call out from their encampment on the grass, but I could not make out what, if anything intelligible, was said. Perhaps the sounds were simple hoots and yells of jocular derision, blank ammunition fired at old age and respectability or the pretentions of high culture. Once or twice I thought I caught the word 'poet' before it was drowned beneath bellows of hilarity. There was one occasion when one of the motor-cyclists shouted something as he roared past but the din from the engine prevented any possibility of my hearing what was said.

All things considered I was finding Berinsfield quite pleasant at that time. Mrs Fitzgerald, my nearest neighbour on the ground floor, would often ask me into her flat for a sherry or coffee and tell me about her daughter who was a nurse in the United States and would soon be coming home, about her grandchildren and – with a mixture of archness, defiance and excited laughter – about her recently-acquired gentleman friend. I now found that I was addressed by name and in a friendly way in most of the shops I used, and in the pub and the club bar I was no longer a strange object of curiosity but an accepted 'regular'. I was on first-name terms with Tony, the Automobile Association patrolman who lived in the flat above me and who, during the winter months, had more than once coaxed my recalcitrant van into starting, doing this, not in his official capacity, but in his spare time, as a friend and neighbour. Ruth and Dot were, if not exactly friends, at least affable acquaintances, these two married – though apparently husbandless at the time – young ladies, both of whom were unlikely aspirants to literary fame and fortune. Roy and Jean were another couple I drank with quite often in The Berinsfield Arms. He was a lugubrious but essentially kind ex-Chief Petty Officer in the Royal Navy and his wife was a devoted reader of historical romances. Other drinking companions included a male nurse who looked after alcoholics in a nearby mental hospital, a prison officer and – for the sake of balance – a recently released ex-convict with no visible means of support. While I had to confess that my didactic or advisory function as Resident Author was not in great demand I thought I noticed a gradually developing interest in my work and life as a writer. I was pleasantly surprised to discover that a few people in the community had gone to the trouble of withdrawing books of mine from the public library and, in some cases, had even read them. Brendan and Jack who, as my first Berinsfield friends, assumed a slightly proprietorial manner, extracted a solemn promise from me that, when my Fellowship ended, I would not lose contact with them, that I would write and would return from time to time when one or other of them would be only too pleased to put me up. The Berinsfield adventure had not, after all, turned out so badly as I had at one time feared.

I was still being kept quite busy visiting schools to give readings. Radley, the public school near Abingdon, invited me, through the Head of the English Department, Peter Way, to attend an event called 'Declamations' and, afterwards, in the evening, give a lecture to sixth-formers on the Poetry of the Two World Wars. Declamations, it was explained to me, was held annually. Every boy in the school was called upon to learn by heart a piece of prose or poetry of his own choice, the passage or complete work to be of a prescribed and quite considerable minimum length, and, in due course, he would publicly recite his chosen item and his performance would be judged by members of the staff. Gradually the very best speakers from each form would be short-listed as finalists until, on Declamations Day, they would stand up before the assembled school and declaim. There were – if I recall correctly – three sections – Junior, Intermediate and Senior – and an eventual winner had to be chosen in each. It was my invidious job to act as sole judge.

The recitations began in the morning; there was a break for lunch and they carried on through the afternoon until about four o'clock. In all I spent about six hours listening to boys of various ages, sizes and degrees of competence speaking lengthy passages in verse or prose. Most of them, sensibly in my opinion since verse is easier to memorize, chose poetry, and the selections were wide-ranging, with a number of surprises, some pleasant and others less so. There was an understandable tendency, especially among the younger boys, to favour light verse, not always of a very high standard (I must have listened to at least half a dozen renderings of 'Albert and the Lion') and, among those who had chosen more serious work, the temptation to over-dramatize was not always resisted. One senior boy chose 'The Love Song of J. Alfred Prufrock'. He knew the entire poem by heart, for which feat of memory alone I was tempted to award him first place, and he spoke the lines with assurance, great clarity and deep feeling. The only trouble was that it was usually the wrong feeling. A simple instance will suffice. He spoke the line 'I have measured out my life with coffee spoons' – this sad, grey little confession of a largely wasted life, timidity's own voice – with tremendous bravura so that it rang out triumphantly in tones more suited to victorious Tamburlaine than mousy little Prufrock.

But generally the standard of verse-speaking was high and I was impressed by the apparent lack of any kind of self-consciousness among the competitors. No one was shy or self-deprecating or embarrassed either by the situation or by his choice of poem or prose. And this, I thought, said a great deal for the school. At the close of Declamations Peter Way and I walked round the playing-fields before going to his house for a meal. We talked about the day's performances and discussed the wisdom of compelling young people to memorize imaginative writing. Ideally, the firm rooting of a poem in the memory should come from repeated readings prompted by pleasure, admiration, love, but not everyone will find sufficient emotional engagement with language for this to happen. In such cases, then, the deliberate committing to memory of a poem could do no harm and could even be a step in the direction of developing the kind of response which would enable spontaneous memorizing to occur. It was true that all of the people I knew who had been forced to learn poetry by heart at school were, in later years, grateful for the little mental anthology they had gathered. But it was also true that, almost without exception, these same people had read no poetry since leaving school.

In the evening I gave my talk to the senior boys and chatted briefly afterwards with members of my audience. They were all pleasant young men showing little or nothing of the awkwardness of so many of the young people I had come across in state schools and, as usual, I was worried by conflicting reactions. These intelligent, reasonably well-read and very courteous young men made my task so much easier and pleasanter to perform. Ahead of them, almost certainly, lay lives of fulfilment. Most of them would be going to university and from there into work which would be satisfying as well as remunerative. Their leisure would be taken up in the pursuit of agreeable and civilized activities. They would enjoy music, books, painting, the theatre. Their homes would be comfortable and aesthetically pleasing, set in pleasant surroundings among other homes and people of the same kind. They would marry intelligent, personable young women. If they played games they would play well, using the best equipment. If they wished to travel they would do so. They were society's chosen few, almost a different species from those boys on the Green in Berinsfield who, no doubt, were whistling and growling at the few girls who ventured out at night, perhaps swigging from can or bottle, belching and guffawing competitively until darkness and the night chill sent them back to bookless, telly-dominated, ugly rooms, the shared bedroom and the prospect of the next long day at factory bench or on building-site. These were the young people I ought really to be talking to, reaching out to offer a hand that might just pull one or two of them out of the quicksands. Yet how could I set about it? Overtures from me would be greeted by jeers and catcalls. And, damn it, it was not my job anyway. I was a writer, not a social worker, missionary or teacher. So, as usual, I ended up by pushing the questions to one side and looking at my watch to see if I could make it to the nearest pub before closing time.

A few days later I drove to Southampton where I was to record a television programme for the BBC Southern network. Over the years I had taken part in quite a few attempts to present poetry on television. The first was in the very early nineteen-sixties when a series called 'Muses with Milligan' was presented by the BBC. The structure of the programme was as follows: Spike Milligan was the centre-piece, compere or anchor-man, and he sat on a high stool wearing a funny hat with a woollen pom-pom; behind him was a jazz ensemble with a sexy black girl singer. Lurking in the background, ready to leap into noisy action, was a folk-singer with a guitar. Milligan recited a few very short whimsical verses of his own composition in the intervals between the jazz and the folk-songs and, half way through the programme, a poet was quickly introduced, permitted a few minutes in which to read a couple of poems, which he and the producer had earlier chosen for their inoffensive accessibility, and then he was whisked away so that the jazz and Spike's Edward Lear-and-water verses could carry the affair to its conclusion.

This kind of apologetic presentation of poetry, sandwiching it between reliably-tested forms of popular entertainment, while arguably harmless, would obviously do nothing to show to an habitually unliterary audience that verse could be enjoyable, could tell them things that they really would be glad to know about and, above all, it could be exciting without the support of anything else – music, sexy girls or funny hats. Later, I was involved in less pussy-footed attempts to present poetry programmes on television, but usually I had the feeling that the producer was afraid that the audience would switch off or switch over to something less intimidating unless they were constantly reassured that the experience was not going to be as painful as their education and prejudices had warned them that it was going to be.

An interesting example of misguided intent to allay audience suspicion and prejudice was provided when, a few years ago, Harlech Television, in an attempt to improve the cultural content of their output decided to risk a poetry reading. Laurie Lee and I were among those taking part and we happened to arrive at the Bristol studio at the same time. A young assistant-producer met us in the foyer of the building. After he had introduced himself he said breezily, 'Well, I think the first thing to do is get you two along to Wardrobe.'

'To what?' Laurie said.

'Wardrobe. You know, get you something a bit more – er – well, suitable to wear.'

'Suitable?'

'Something more ... well, let's face it. You don't look like poets, either of you. Not what people expect poets to look like.'

I asked him exactly what he had in mind: bardic robes, perhaps? Tennysonian cloak and wide brimmed hat? Or Eliot-style city gent's costume?

'Oh no, nothing like that. Leather jackets and jeans, I thought. Casual. You know the kind of thing.'

'Yes,' Laurie said grimly, 'I know the kind of thing. Now, you listen to me. I've looked like a yard-and-a-half of old knitting for many, many years and I haven't the slightest intention of changing now. So please let's go along to the studio, shall we?'

We got along to the studio, unpoetically clad as we were.

The Southampton programme was the most congenial I had

so far been involved in. Brian Thompson, the interviewer, asked the kind of questions that gave me a chance to talk about what I believed to be important and the producer was remarkably un-assertive and content to leave the choice of poems to me. After the recording the three of us had lunch in a pub and then I drove back to Oxfordshire.

There was some mail waiting for me on the hall floor: a letter from a lady enclosing some poems written by her nine-year-old son, an invitation to read at an International Summer School to be held at Exeter College and a slightly heavier package which turned out to be a paperback volume of poems by an old Leeds friend of mine, privately published by his widow after his recent and shockingly unexpected death from a heart-attack.

My friend's name was Kenneth Severs and we had first met in Leeds about thirty years earlier. For two years or so we had been very close companions and then our lives had moved apart and we saw each other less and less frequently. Except for a short period when he lectured at Hatfield College, Durham, he had stayed in Leeds, first working for the BBC and then, towards the end of his life, returning to teaching in the English School of his local university. When I lived in London we would meet each time he had occasion to visit the Capital but, after my marriage and departure for the South-West, even these irregular meetings ceased and the bond that existed between us was stretched to a fine thread. Yet it was always there. It never snapped or disintegrated.

I made myself a pot of tea and sat down with Kenneth's poems. I could hear, from outside, the shouts of children calling to each other in the sunlight, exultant in their release from school. The tea tasted good. I could smell its fragrance as I started to read. At once I knew that I could not possibly form an objective opinion of the merits of the work. A number of the poems I already knew well. Some had been written in our shared Leeds days and I felt something of the almost paternal, indulgent affection for them that one occasionally feels for one's own juvenilia. A few I had seen on their publication in magazines and those which I had not read before were recognizably in Kenneth's style and idiom, a fastidious yet romantic voice, a heavy sense of indebtedness to Yeats, Eliot and the early Auden, a strong feeling for tradition and con-siderable skill in working in complex forms such as the sestina

129

and canzone. Whatever else they might be these poems were not negligible, yet the little book seemed pitifully slender testimony to a life's work. He had never received much in the way of public recognition and here, it seemed, was his total output, less than seventy pages of rather poor typography abounding in printer's errors; not much to leave behind for a man whose devotion to his art was uncompromising.

I remembered the early days of our friendship when we would show each other our poems and make plans for the time when we would move away from the restricting climate of the industrial north, go south and storm the literary metropolis. But, for the time being, Leeds was as good a place as any, and better than most. We would meet in The Pack Horse or Whitelocks or The Victoria where we might be joined by Jacob Kramer, the painter, or by Wilfred Childe, who lectured in English at the University, and we would discuss our latest enthusiasms and Kenneth would probably, for the hundreth time, outline a scheme for starting a literary magazine that would be regional yet whose contents would surpass in quality those of any other journal in the country. We would quote to each other from our favourite poets, argue their relative merits, disagreeing with vehemence and agreeing with delight. It was a time of conscious growth. I could actually trace the deepening understanding, was aware of its development in the way that a woman must be aware of the growing child inside her. New experiences, in the arts and in the life of the mind generally, were seasoned by our hunger and curiosity and our appetites seemed insatiable.

I thought of other friends and acquaintances of those days, of Bonamy Dobrée, the Professor of English at Leeds and sympathetic and helpful friend to both Kenneth and me, almost a parody of the dandy and the scholar, in whose company I always felt uncouth and clumsy, but a fine teacher who cared deeply for both his subject and for those of his students in whom he might glimpse a reflection of his own passion for the literature of the eighteenth century. Then there was Bernard Brett, wry and melancholy author of a single novel, written years before I met him, now incapable of doing anything except drift from bar to bar in search of something that he had not only lost but could no longer quite recall. Bernard was unusual in that he was one of the few deeply depressed people who was not himself depressing company. His profound sympathy, his deep instinctive courtesy, would not allow him to transmit his disease and he prevented this from happening by the exercise of an inventive, self-mocking wit.

Another Leeds friend of that time was Henry Webber, Catholic apostate and a pianist who played with more passion than musicianship but whose love and reverence for the great composers and their work could not have been more deeply felt by the most lavishly-gifted virtuoso. It was Henry who, at a party where music was being discussed in a not particularly well-informed manner, was the cause of acute embarrassment to his hostess and to some of the more gently nurtured guests: a rather affected and loud-voiced lady was extolling the accomplishments of a well-known female pianist, who was perhaps more richly endowed with dress-sense than musical ability, when Henry, who had drunk more deeply than wisely, burst out with: 'Don't talk to me about women pianists! You need a pair of balls to play Beethoven!'

Jacob and Wilfred, Bonamy, Bernard, Henry and now Kenneth, all dead. And what was left of them in the world of the living? They would stay around for a time, prowling the dark side-streets of the memory, every now and then would come into view, seen sharply, summoned by a trick of the senses, a scent, a sound, a snatch of music perhaps, the taste of a drink or a certain kind of tobacco. Dobrée, I supposed, had earned his little niche in the history of eighteenth-century literary scholarship; there must be a few of Jacob's paintings around, somewhere, and they might still give pleasure to their owners; I doubted if anyone read Wilfred's ornate devotional verses or Bernard's solitary novel which must have been out of print for years; however vigorously Henry had pounded the keys his music had faded into silence now; Kenneth's single volume of poems, *A Place of Being,* would stay on my shelves until the time for my bell of quittance came round and, after that, who could say what would become of it. Scholarship, painting, music and literature would go on; that was the only consolation, and a pretty thin comfort to offer the personally bereaved.

I thought it was time to make a real effort to banish the gathering shades of despondency. I put Kenneth's book away, gathered up the tea-things, washed and dried them and put them away. Then I went out and drove into Oxford to visit a

131

friend in Southmoor Road who owned a fine record player and collection of records. A couple of drinks in a pub on the way, a bottle of wine to carry away and then a long cool draught of Mozart, that is what I needed to keep the old *timor mortis* at a distance. And that is what I had, and it worked tolerably well.

The next evening, a Friday, I went to Whitchurch, a small village on the Thames, adjoining Pangbourne, where a poetry-reading was being held in the local school. I was not taking an active part, but it was organized by John Loveday who was a member of the Southern Arts Literature Panel and for whom I had given a number of readings in the past and, since he had gone out of his way to invite me to attend and since the two poets who were reading were both old friends as well as writers whose work I respected, I thought it well worth the expense of time and effort on a visit.

It proved to be an enjoyable occasion. John Loveday had booked a jazz group to play during the interval and after the poetry-reading was over, and the large audience seemed well pleased with the evening's entertainment. Later that night I went to a party given by a young couple whom I had met on previous visits to the area, Peter and Diana Mottley, and I spent the night with them after it had prudently been decided that I would be ill-advised to drive back to Berinsfield. On the Saturday morning I felt rather better than I had expected or deserved to feel and, after a couple of beers and some lunch in the Ferryboat Inn, I set off on my journey back to Berinsfield.

The summer had by now got into its stride. There had been no rain for some weeks and the pastureland was beginning to look dehydrated, drained of colour, and here and there you could see charred, black sections where fires had raged. Older people were saying that this was a real summer, like those they remembered as kids, summers that started in April or May and went on and on, heat-soaked day after day, until the autumn's gentle intercession. Berinsfield was powdered by fine dust and was pungent with melted tar and petrol fumes. Inside the flat it was comparatively cool but still too warm for complete comfort. I sat at my window which overlooked the Green, the parade of shops and the pub, and I read through some of the letters that were waiting to be answered. But I could not summon up the energy and the mental concentration to write replies so I stayed there, staring out at the almost empty street and the Green which, unusually for a weekend, was also deserted. Then I heard children's voices and I saw that three boys of nine or ten were passing the window, each of them carrying a rolled towel.

I thought I recognized them as members of one of my audiences at the Abbey Junior School. I opened the window and called, 'Hullo! You going swimming?'

They stopped, surprised for a moment, then one of them said, 'Yes, we're going to the pond.'

'What pond? Where is it?'

'Just by the Little Chef. At the back. It's a smashing place for swimming.'

The Little Chef was an eating-house next to a large garage and filling-station which faced the exit from Berinsfield onto the main road to Oxford.

One of the boys said, 'If you want to go, you'll see a gap in the hedge about twenty yards down from the garage. You go through that and you'll see a small pond. It's not that one. It's the next, a big 'un. They sail there, on the other side. It's great.'

I thanked the boys and they continued on their way. I stayed at the window for a while, staring at the Green which was now mocked by its name. Heat shimmered over the yellowing coarse grass that was clipped and spare, penitential. The sight of it made me feel thirsty. I looked at my watch. It was nearly four o'clock. At least three more hours of extreme warmth. I made up my mind. A swim would be wonderful. It would be good exercise, yet cool and refreshing, and what slight traces of hangover remained would soon be dispelled. I found my swimming-trunks and shoved them into a carrier-bag along with a bath towel and a copy of the *World's Classics Letters of John Keats*. Then I left the flat and drove the few hundred yards to the main road, parked on the grass verge opposite the promised gap in the hedge, left the van and squeezed through the aperture and saw, through foliage, a small expanse of water glittering in the sunlight. I pushed my way through the branches to the edge of the pool and walked on to the next, much larger one, in which a dozen or so people, mainly children – though there were two or three older youths and their girls – were disporting themselves. A small diving-board had been erected in the shallows of the pool so, clearly, swimming was not forbidden. I found a comfortable and secluded spot on the bank, undressed and put on my trunks. Then I went to the diving-board and plunged into the water.

I stayed in for about a quarter of an hour then got out, dried myself and, still in my trunks, settled down to read for a while. I had felt a little uneasy about trespassing on what seemed to be a preserve of the young but no one had taken the least notice of me and now I felt quite at ease. This place was a splendid discovery. I could envisage the hot weather going on for a long time yet, probably for the whole of the two months I had still to spend in Berinsfield, and this haven should make that period not just bearable but positively enjoyable. I had always been fond of swimming and I certainly needed the exercise. The demands on my time imposed by the Fellowship were becoming less onerous. I could foresee days spent on the banks of the natural pool, reading and perhaps writing, gradually extending the duration and strenuousness of my daily swim, becoming sun-tanned, trim of waist and clear-eyed.

After an hour or so of reading I got dressed and went back to the flat. There I ate some salad and corned beef and then, feeling smugly virtuous, I sat down and answered the letters that earlier I had felt unable to deal with. By the time the last envelope was sealed, addressed and stamped I decided that I had earned a drink. I collected together the mail, made sure that I had got the key to the flat and money for drinks, and went out into the still golden yet less strident heat of the evening. It was not a bad life and there were far worse places to be in than Berinsfield.

As I crossed the road to the pub I heard the noise of the youngsters, who by now had assembled on the Green, as they argued, wrestled and taunted one another. There was a louder shout followed by a volley of guffaws. I thought I heard the word 'poet'. Then quite distinctly the name 'Scannell' was shouted, followed by more loud merriment. I looked across to where they were sitting, standing or sprawling on the grass, and I waved cordially. They were suddenly silent, but only for a moment, after which there came another outburst of laughter and some comments which, at that distance, I could not attach any meaning to. I paused for a few seconds. They were all watching me, but were quieter now. Then I waved to them again and went into the pub.

134

EIGHT

THE HEAT-WAVE BECAME an engulfing flood. There were
reports in the newspapers and on the radio and television of
serious shortages of water in parts of the South-West where
strict rationing had been introduced; gardeners complained
that their vegetable crops were dying from too much sun and
too little moisture; the price of potatoes soared. In the streets of
Oxford everyone, except a few of the old or inflexibly conven-
tional, wore as little clothing as was decently possible. The
pubs sold huge quantities of chilled lager and everywhere you
could smell a curious mixture of sweat, sun-tan lotion and
burning rubber. It was exciting, erotic weather, and obscurely
dangerous. We were not used to this unremitting heat. Beneath
the festive glitter, the holiday abandoment, moved a nervous
undertow, an unformed threat.

The schools would soon be breaking up for the long vacation.
I made a return visit to Banbury Comprehensive, spending an
entire day there, working with different age-groups, and I
found, at the end of it, that my faith in the system had been at
least partially restored. What was confirmed, if confirmation
were needed, was the conviction that by far the most important
factor in education, infinitely more important than facilities,
buildings, décor and theories, was good teaching, the serious,
inquisitive, knowledgeable, humble and profound love of the
thing being taught and the gift of transmitting that love. A good
deal of this was to be found at Banbury.

Back in Berinsfield I went regularly to the pool. I would take
with me bread, cheese and fruit and a couple of cans of beer
which I would place in the water to keep relatively cool until I
was ready to drink them. After my swim I would lie in the sun
until the heat became uncomfortable and then I would find
shade beneath a tree and prop myself up in a position for
reasonably painless reading. I even, on occasion, did a little
writing. I had never found it easy to work out of doors. The
sense of movement, the sounds, the quality of the light, were all
effective distractions, but, as I grew more accustomed to them, I
found that I was able to increase the duration of the periods of
work. So these were good days, and I ought to be looking back
to them with affection, but I cannot do so because of the events

that followed, darkening and infecting with their spreading virus the purity of what should and could have been a modest idyll.

It all began quietly, so tentative at first that I was not sure of its nature, even inclined to take it for what was in truth its opposite, for friendliness, for a clumsy gesture of acceptance. But those boys on the Green were not offering friendship. Their cries and whistles and hoots, increasing steadily in volume, whenever I appeared in the street, were anything but friendly. There could be no doubting that their jeers were contemptuous and hostile, and, as their campaign warmed up, it became easier to distinguish among the animal noises, actual words. 'Poet!' they would shout, and there was no mistaking the hatred and derision in their voices. Then one evening, as I crossed the road to The Berinsfield Arms, I heard four or five of them chanting, '*Scann*-ell! *Scann*-ell! He's a poet and he don't know it!' This witty piece of choral-speaking was followed by a bellow and screech of laughter and then a single, very loud voice shouted: 'He aint a poet, he's a silly old cunt!' and there was another, even greater, explosion of hysterical laughter.

I stopped and looked across at them. I felt sick with rage. My first impulse was to go across to them, grab one, any one, and knock the shit out of him. But reason was functioning just enough to be able to counsel against this course. If I started to move towards them they would probably scatter and I would be left looking helpless, frustrated and silly. Or, if they did not run away, would I really, when it came to it, pick on one at random? If I did it would probably be the wrong one, the least offensive, a sheepish follower. No, I would have to wait, to make some enquiries, try to find out who the leader was, for I was sure the solo shouter, the one with the biggest voice, was the one.

When I paused the noise quietened almost to silence but, as I turned away and walked towards the pub, it rose again, louder, if anything, than before, a taunting howl, scornful, brutal and loathsome.

Brendan was at the bar. I must have looked shaken because at once he said, 'Hello, what's wrong? You look a bit – you had bad news or something?'

I ordered a pint.

'What's the matter with you, Vernon? You not feeling well?'

I said, 'Did you hear that row? Those kids on the Green?'

136

'Yeah, I heard something. What was it about then?'

'Me. They were yelling at me.' I realized as I spoke that I probably sounded petulant, absurd, pomposity comically deflated, and I would not have been surprised if Brendan had laughed at me. But he did not laugh.

'What they do that for?'

I shrugged.

'Maybe they didn't mean no harm. They're just kids. They want their backsides skelping.'

I felt better after a drink. 'They'll get more than that if they keep it up.'

'Ah, no. You don't want to let the likes of them worry you. Take no notice. They'll soon get fed up with it. Have another pint. Forget 'em. They're not worth bothering about.'

Of course Brendan was right. It was a disturbing sign of my own immaturity that I should be so shaken by what was at worst a display of ignorant prejudice and bad manners from youngsters who, considering their environment, could not be held responsible for either. It was natural that they should resent the presence of someone who, by their standards and those of their elders, did no useful work yet was given a free flat in the village when they and their fathers had to pay rent which had to be earned by hard graft with pick and shovel or on the assembly line. In their eyes I was an elderly layabout, posh, arty, probably a pouf, a natural target for their frustrated and puzzled anger. Obviously I must ignore their demonstrations and hope that, as Brendan had promised, they would soon look elsewhere for their entertainment.

When we left the pub at closing-time the youngsters were still on the Green. There were no shouts but I sensed that they were watching us carefully and I could hear a low mutter of comment.

We stopped outside my flat.

Brendan said, 'I don't think they'll give you any more trouble. They know me.' He spoke with some satisfaction. They would not dare to try it on him. And he was right. He was someone known and respected, and he was in a sense one of them.

We said goodnight and I went indoors, switched on the lights and drew the curtains. I filled the kettle and put it on the gas to make some coffee before going to bed. A little light music, I told myself, would be an excellent palliative for my bruised sensibilities and who better to supply it than Mozart himself. I was searching among my cassettes for the Piano Concerto No 27 in B flat major when I was startled by a sudden loud banging on the window of the living-room, four or five thumps, so heavy that it was a wonder the glass did not shatter. For a second I was paralyzed; then I sprang to the windows and pulled back the curtains but, though I must have been clearly and ridiculously visible to anyone outside, I could see only the silhouettes of the church tower on the Green and the roofs of the houses beyond it. I readjusted the curtains and went into the hall and listened. Then, careful not to make any sound, I opened the door and tiptoed out of the flat, through the vestibule to the outer entrance and into the street. I stayed in the shadows close to the building. There were distant sounds of traffic from the main road and, nearer but still out of sight, a motor-cycle started up and roared away. I waited, but saw or heard nothing of my young friends. Yet I felt that someone was still there, perhaps hiding in the shop doorways on the Parade, watching me.

The sick, tremulous feeling of anger had come back just as strongly. My mouth was dry and I was sweating. I wanted to hurt somebody. Presently the tension eased a little and I went back into the flat. My kettle had boiled dry and the kitchen was full of steam. I swore, turned off the gas and decided that I could not be bothered to heat more water. I switched off the lights in the kitchen and living-room and went into the bedroom, undressed and climbed between the sheets. Maybe I would feel better in the morning, more able to view the situation calmly. I might even be able to find out the names of one or two of the kids and have a word with their parents. One thing I was sure about. I was not going to let a handful of half-baked delinquents spoil my last few weeks in Berinsfield. I gave the pillows an unnecessarily hard thump and composed myself for sleep. But quite a long time passed before it came.

I went for a swim the next morning and, in the afternoon, I drove into Oxford to have tea with an elderly lady who had written to me asking if I would call on her to read her poems and perhaps give her some advice. She lived in a pleasant little house in a street close to the Radcliffe Infirmary and, as soon as I arrived, she sat me down with a folder containing her poems while she busied herself making tea and preparing neat little sandwiches of cream cheese and cucumber. I saw at once that her work was of the kind most difficult to discuss because it was, in a sense, beyond criticism, or beyond any kind that would be of practical help to her. Each poem was quite lucid, fluently written in regular metre and rhyme, and all of them were devotional, reminding me a little of George Herbert, but wholely lacking his formal invention, wit, and freshness of image. The trouble was the one common with older practitioners of such verse: the vocabulary and idiom she employed were those of a time remote from the present; the poems were as lifeless as paper flowers.

Over tea I tried to explain some of this to her as gently as I could, but I could sense immediately her resentment and suspicion.

She said, 'You mean they aren't Modern,' and her emphasis on and pronunciation of the word 'Modern' made it clear that she regarded it as a term of opprobrium.

We looked at each other over the sandwiches and pretty china. I was the enemy. I thought of the yobs on the Green howling for my blood and this old lady who, I was quite sure, would not need much more provocation to empty the teapot over my head, and I felt a twinge of self-pity.

She said, 'The thing I read about you in the library said it was part of your job to help people to get their work published.'

I shook my head. 'If that's what is said, it had no right to. Getting work published is a publisher's job or an agent's. I haven't got the slightest influence in that way. All I can advise you to do is get the *Writers' and Artists' Year Book* and you'll find there a list of all the publishers in the country along with the kind of thing they specialize in and so on. There's no way except sending off your work and hoping someone somewhere, sooner or later, will like it enough to publish it.'

'That's not very helpful.'

'No, I'm sorry.'

'Well, I suppose it was foolish of me to expect much help from someone like you.'

I wondered briefly what she meant by someone like me, but I thought it wiser not to enquire. I stood up. 'I really must go now. I'm sorry I've been so unhelpful. Thank you for the tea.'

She saw me to the door, her face set in unforgiving lines. Out in the sunshine I released a deeply indrawn breath which I had not been aware of holding. Then, as soon as the first relief and embarrassment faded, I began to feel guilty. Surely I could have found some way of giving her hope. It had not been necessary to tell her the truth. Anyone with an ounce of charity in them would have found a way of giving her encouragement of some kind. All I had done was take away what little hope she might have been hanging on to. I had been inconsiderate and lazy. I ought to have been prepared for the kind of work she would show and have had my comforting answers ready. The next time – if there was to be one, and I hoped to God there was not – I would lie my head off, say what was wanted, not what was true.

I was back in Berinsfield at about six o'clock. The Green was deserted. It was too early for the evening assembly to have gathered. I parked the van and went into the flat, put the *Four Last Songs* of Richard Strauss on to my cassette-player and started to try and tidy the place up, but I was soon sweating from my mild exertions and I flopped down into a chair and lit a cigarette. Before long I heard the first signs of the teen-age conclave forming outside, the splutter and growl of motor-cycle engines, shouts and the mindless, honking laughter that I was beginning to detest with a quite disproportionate rage. I tried hard to calm myself, to exercise reason and tolerance: I had told myself often enough that youngsters like these were victims of a cruelly inegalitarian society and an educational system that had failed them, and here I was, reacting to a bit of teasing like an irate Justice of the Peace. But when I looked out of the window and saw them gathering like birds of prey I felt nothing but distaste and an obscure fear.

A little later I went out of the flat and set off across the road to the pub. I had not gone more than ten yards before the caterwauling and jeers and hoots began. A section of them began to chant my name like a football crowd: '*Scann* -ell . . . *Scann* -ell . . . *Scann* -ell!' Then: '*Po* -et . . . *Po* -et . . . *Po* -et . . . *Po* -et!' I walked grimly on. I had almost reached the entrance to The Berinsfield Arms when something whizzed past my head. I stopped and looked back towards the Green and saw that one of the boys had left the main group and come forward to the edge of the Green so that he could be in range to hurl an apple-core at me. He was quite tall, with long fair hair. I thought I would be able to distinguish him from the others when the time came.

Inside the pub Brendan was waiting at the bar.

'Jesus,' he said. 'It was you they was getting at! I heard them. The little bastards.'

I ordered drinks. 'Yes, it was me all right. But I'll fix them. I know one of them now. A biggish lad. Long blond hair. Do you know him?'

'I might if I saw him.'

'Come out and have a look.'

The drinks were put on the counter and I paid for them.

Brendan shook his head. 'No. Don't start anything. If we go over there you're going to clobber one of them. Then what happens? You're in trouble. Assault. It's happened before. There was a fellow in the place Jack lives in. Ground floor flat like yours. He had the same trouble. Worse. They smashed his windows. Gave him and his wife a helluva time. And what happens. He gets hold of one of the little bastards and gives him a bit of a tanning. The kid goes home bawling his eyes out, says he's been beaten up. Dad goes round to play hell and by this time your man's had enough and he puts one on Dad's chin. Round come the coppers. And who's the criminal? Not the kids. Not the ones that've smashed the windows and given the poor man a dog's life. Not at all. It's your man. He's the guilty one. He's the law-breaker. And they give him a suspended sentence for assault and twenty quid costs.'

'It would be worth it.'

'Now you're talking daft, man. I know how you feel but use the loaf. Think what you're doing. It's light now. There's witnesses. You want to fix it so's you can get this one on his own. In the dark. No witnesses. Then he can squeal his head off but there's no proof. And there's another thing. There's a dozen or more of 'em over there now. You grab one and the rest of 'em will be on you. Okay, you can handle a couple, three maybe, but not a dozen of the bastards. And some of them's hefty kids. And vicious. Maybe got knives. You got to box clever, Vernon. Anyway, they'll soon get fed up and look for somebody else.'

I was not convinced.

A little later Jack came in and we stayed there until the pub closed. When we left, the group was still on the Green. There were no shouts until we reached the entrance to the flats and I had stopped to exchange goodnights with Brendan and Jack.

141

Then a single, very loud voice bawled: '*Scann*-ell! *Po* -et! Doesn't fuckin' know it! Silly old bastard! *Sca-a-a-nn*-ell!'

I said, 'Right!' and started off in the direction of the youths.

Brendan grabbed my arm. 'Hang on! Don't be a bloody fool!'

But any possibility of my being able to exercise self-control had been washed away by the alcohol I had swallowed and I shook him off, crossed the Green, and advanced on my tormentors. Brendan followed with Jack at a safe distance behind him. He caught up with me.

'Now take it easy,' he muttered. 'Keep the head.'

As I approached, some of the boys who had been sitting on the turf rose slowly to their feet. Others stayed where they were, watching. They were all silent now.

I said, 'Who's the one doing the shouting?'

No one answered. They remained still and watchful. I looked from face to face but, in the darkness, I could not be sure that the blond youth was among them.

Brendan said, 'They're just stupid kids. Don't know any better. Don't bother yourself with them. Let's go. They're not worth it.'

I could feel my heart thumping, my fists had involuntarily bunched into knuckled weapons.

'Come on,' I said, 'which one of you? Who's the big brave boy who does the shouting?' I knew that no one was going to speak and I had to get away with what little dignity I could salvage. 'All right. Just as I thought. I knew you gutless little shits'd all be too scared to own up. Now you listen to me, all of you. If there's any more of this yelling my name or anything else – any more banging on my windows – any trouble of any kind from now on – I'll pick the nearest one I can get my hands on and he'll wish he'd never been born. I'll fillet him. I'll pulp the bastard. You got it?' My anger was being fed by my own rhetoric. I wanted to take a smack at one of them before I left.

'All right, Vernon,' Brendan said. 'They've got the message. Let's go.'

We turned and walked away from the gang. There were no shouts, no sounds at all from them.

Back at the entrance to the flats Brendan said, 'I think you put the wind up them. You'll not be hearing any more now.'

I hoped he was right. My heady charge of aggression, part

142

authentic, part simulated, had died down. Indoors I got ready for bed. I knew that I had put on an act out there on the Green, or, more accurately, there had been an element of conscious histrionics in my exhibition; the verbal threats and curses had voiced a genuine violence but the anger, though real enough, had put on fancy-dress. I now felt a little ashamed but I could not regret my display if it were going to prove effective in silencing my band of young enemies. The whole incident seemed to be melancholy proof that the only effective means of maintaining order, of de-fusing the destructive forces in a society, was through coercion, through counter-threats of greater violence. Sweet reasonableness, appeals to good sense or nature, would not have diverted these boys one inch from their course of harassment. But the threat of having their teeth kicked in had pulled them up in their tracks.

I switched the lights off and got into bed. Ten seconds later there was a mighty banging on the living-room windows and a chorus of wordless howls from outside. First, disbelief held me motionless, then a moment of despair before I leaped out of bed, hit my knee painfully on a chair as I dashed for the light, staggered through to the living-room and swung back the curtains. I thought I caught a glimpse of a figure disappearing into the darkness, but I could not be sure. I slipped my trousers on and put my bare feet into sandals. Then I switched off all the lights in the flat and went swiftly and quietly out to the shadowed place where I had lurked on the previous night. I crouched there, keeping perfectly still, listening. A car went past, its headlights defining quite plainly the church and the patch of Green where the youngsters usually congregated, but there was no one there. When the sound of the car's engine had died away there was a silence which I searched carefully for the least sound. There was none. I waited and waited but there was no sign of anyone abroad in the night. Twenty minutes must have passed before I realized I was going to be frustrated again. I stayed for another five and then went back into the flat.

I sat in the kitchen in the darkness. By then it was past midnight, too late, surely, for any further interruption. Somehow I would have my revenge. They were not going to get away with it. I had done them no harm, had not shown any ill-will towards them. Why should they subject me to their persecution? The next day, in broad daylight, witnesses or no witnesses, I would

143

get one of them and show him and his friends that I meant everything I had threatened. But now I had better get some sleep if my jangling nerves would permit it. I went back to the bedroom, kicked off my sandals and was just stepping out of my trousers when I heard a sound from the hall. Then a voice – *the* voice – the oafish, thick, bullying voice of my chief tormentor inside the flat, in the hall, bellowed: 'Scannell! Old cunt! Poet! Silly old cunt!'

Holding my trousers at the waist I dashed through the living-room, fumbled for the switch in the hall. As the lights came on I heard a click from the door. It was the letter-box. He had been shouting through the letter-box. Bare-footed, I snatched open the door and ran through the vestibule into the street. But I knew the chase was hopeless. They had won another round. But it would be their last victory, I swore to that. They would not get away with any more.

I slept late the next day, a Friday, and it was almost noon by the time I had bathed, shaved and dressed. I was drinking coffee and eating cheese biscuits when the telephone rang. It was Lincoln Kirstein who had just arrived in London. He had come mainly for the celebrations of Madame Rambert's fifty years' promotion of British ballet.

He said, 'Any chance you might be in London? It'd be good to see you. How about lunch tomorrow? I'm at the Connaught.'

I did not hesitate. 'Tommorrow's fine. I'll be there at one.'

'Great. Look forward to seeing you.'

After I had put the telephone down I realized that my immediate acceptance had been prompted as much by the wish to escape from Berinsfield and the conflict with the teenage gang as by the desire to see Lincoln, genuine though that desire was. It meant that I could retreat honourably. I would not have been driven away. And, since I had to be at the Connaught the following day at lunch-time, it would obviously be easier for me to travel to London today and spend the night there. So I rang Peter Porter to make sure that he could give me a bed for the night, or perhaps a little longer; then I went over to The Berinsfield Arms and left a message for Brendan telling him that I had been called away unexpectedly on business and would see him when I returned on Sunday or Monday. Back in the flat I packed a bag and let myself out into the vestibule. Mrs Fitzgerald was at the door of her apartment.

'Oh, Mr Scallon,' she said, 'I'm glad I've caught you. I thought I ought to tell you. I woke up very early this morning and you know my kitchen looks out onto where you park your car. Well, I got up, as I say, very early, and I was making myself a cup of tea and I looked out of the window and there was somebody doing something to your car. Something to the wheels. I thought I'd better tell you in case there's any damage. It was one of those Hell's Angels or whatever they call them. He'd got one of those black leather jackets and he rode off on a motor-bike.'

'Was he dark or fair?'

'I couldn't really say. He'd got one of those hats on, what-you-call-them, motor-bike hats, helmets.'

I thanked her and said I would go and see if he had done any damage. Then I went out to the van. Neatly positioned beneath each tyre was the base and the jagged shard of a smashed beer-bottle. They were tucked inconspicuously under the wheels and I would not have noticed their presence had I not been warned. Almost certainly all four tyres would have been punctured if I had tried to drive away. I picked the lumps of glass up and threw them into the dustbin in the yard at the back of the flats. Mrs Fitzgerald was still hovering in the vestibule. I thanked her again and told her about the sabotage of my van.

She said, 'You've been having a bit of trouble, haven't you? I heard them last night. They're the ones that give Berinsfield such a bad name. And no one seems to be able to do anything about it. I mean, their parents don't have any control and the police won't help. The vicar tried to get the police in when they broke into the church but they weren't really interested.'

'I didn't know about the church.'

'Oh yes. That was – what? – two or three months ago. I do the flowers, you see, and I went to unlock the church on Sunday morning but the door was already open. And inside! Oh, Mr Scallon, I couldn't tell you what horrible things they'd done. Filthy beasts. *And* they'd drunk the communion wine.'

As I drove out of Berinsfield I felt a sense of liberation that was almost physical, as if I were literally moving out of an atmosphere that was polluted into cleaner air that held no threat, and by the time I reached London, I could survey the situation more calmly. I told myself that I must not allow those youths to force me to play their game, and that was what had begun to happen. I had been responding to their harassment in exactly the way they wanted, by throwing tantrums of impotent fury, countering obscenity with obscenity and providing them with a rare comic spectacle. The rage and aggression they had aroused in me were alarming, as was their power to engender them. In future I must stay in control, watch the patterns of their behaviour and, if their campaign continued, I would bring in the police and make sure they were witnesses of the boys' behaviour at its worst.

The weekend did a lot to restore my equanimity and I drove back to Berinsfield on the Monday morning feeling quite cheerful but, as soon as I came into sight of the place itself, I could not prevent a lowering of the spirits and, again, I had the feeling of breathing a different air, impure, dangerous. The weather was still relentlessly hot and I would have liked to have gone for a swim but I was booked to give a reading in the afternoon at a school in Oxford called Rye Saint Anthony; so I drove into Abingdon, had lunch there, and went on to the school. After the reading the Head of English, a pleasant and intelligent woman, gave me tea in her house and, as we sat talking, I knew that I was protracting my stay because I feared returning to Berinsfield. And, later, I delayed my return further by going for a leisurely walk round Oxford and calling in at a couple of pubs, so it was approaching nine o'clock and the glitter of day had faded to a wistful mistiness when I parked the van outside The Berinsfield Arms.

I had already seen the group on their usual patch on the Green. I switched off the engine and sat for a moment, considering whether I should go and speak to them, coolly, without anger, asking them for the last time to stop their games with me. It might be worth a try. I got out of the van and started to walk towards them. Instantly they released a barrage of hoots, cat-calls and yells in my direction and I at once turned back and withdrew to the temporary refuge of the pub.

Brendan nodded briefly as I joined him and I could see straight away that he was not in a cheerful mood.

I said, 'Those kids are at it again.'

He nodded but said nothing.

I waited until the drinks had been served. 'They came back

that night, Thursday. And they – or one of them – tried to puncture my tyres.'

'Where've you been?'

'I had to give a talk in Oxford this afternoon.'

'I don't mean today. The weekend.'

'I went to London. Someone I had to see.'

'Just as well you did.'

Something was troubling him. 'Why?'

'You might have got mixed up in the bit of bother I had, Saturday night.'

'With the same lot? The kids?'

'No.' His tone was contemptuous, plainly indicating that a few teen-agers were not likely to present him with any problems. 'No, there was a dance at the club. I got into an argument. Somebody thought he was a hard man. Insulted me, he did. We went outside but he give his mates the nod, didn't he. Four of the bastards followed us out. One of my mates got the word to Mel – he was in the dancing – and he comes out to shorten the odds a bit. Then what do you think one of the bastards does? Only pushes a bottle in Mel's face. Ten stitches he needed. I'll get the bastard that did it, I swear to God I'll get him.'

More senseless violence; it seemed to be in the air you breathed.

I said, 'How did it start? What was the trouble about in the first place?'

Brendan looked annoyed, as if I had asked a stupid, irrelevant question. 'I told you. He insulted me.'

I suspected that Brendan had no very clear memory of why the fracas had begun so I did not pursue the matter.

After another couple of drinks he cheered up a little, though every now and then he would mutter dark promises of the vengeance he would wreak on Mel's assailant.

As closing-time drew near he said, 'You was on about those kids. They been after you again?'

I told him about the shouts through the letter-box.

'Maybe you could catch him. Set a trap.'

'Maybe.' I was not optimistic.

'Yeah. If you acted like you was going home. Go inside, put all the lights on, then nip smartly out into the entrance-hall. You could hide under the stairs there. When the bugger comes in to get at your letter-box you grab him.'

I had myself thought of doing something of the kind. The main argument against it was my uncertainty about what would ensue if I did catch my prey. If he fought to free himself I would either have to let him go or use greater violence to restrain him. I had little doubt that I would be capable of handling him; what worried me was the depth of my anger, the likelihood of my going berserk and inflicting on him more damage than was necessary.

Brendan seemed to sense that I had reservations. 'Listen,' he said, 'let's leave it for tonight. I want to be back early to see the film of the Stracey fight. Why don't we get a couple of bottles and you come back with me? You'd like to see the fight, wouldn't you? The missus'll fix us a bit of supper. Bread and cheese and pickles. We'll watch the box, have a bit of a crack, a couple of jars, and when you get home the kids will have buggered off to bed. Then tomorrow night we can fix 'em. That sound okay?' So when we left the pub we got straight into the van and quickly drove off to the other end of the village where Brendan lived and the boys on the Green were cheated of their sport for that night.

I did not get back to the flat until well after midnight and, if the youths had continued their campaign, I was not aware of it. I slept deeply but, when I awoke I did not feel refreshed. My head ached, eyes were bloodshot and my mouth was sour and dry. It felt like a hangover or like that unpleasant state after an all-night train or boat journey with no sleep and too many cigarettes; yet I had not drunk nearly enough with Brendan to warrant such a condition. It was as if the spiritual sickness in the air was affecting me physically. I drank some orange-juice and a mug of coffee but did not feel much better. The sun was pounding out the heat from a clear sky. It was going to be another scorching day. I had no appointments so the most sensible and agreeable thing to do was to go for a swim.

I collected together my swimming gear, chose a book – it was a paperback novel that would not make any demands – and left the flat. I drove to the main road and parked the van in the usual place. I was beginning to feel more cheerful at the prospect of being immersed in cool water. I crossed to the gap in the hedge

148

and stopped abruptly. It had been closed up by barbed wire. I walked along the side of the road, looking for another gap, but I could not find one. My swim became more desirable than ever now that it looked as if I was to be cheated of it. I could not think why the entrance to the pool should have been blocked unless the land was private property which had recently fallen into new and kill-joy hands. Damn it, I thought, I will get through that hedge somehow.

I went back to the van and dug out an old travelling-rug, which I kept in the back, and I carried this over to the wired-up entrance to the pool. I draped the rug over the wire, threw my swimming things to the other side of the hedge and laboriously heaved myself after them, sustaining a few scratches on the way, but breathlessly triumphant at having breached the defences. The rug had become tangled up in the wire and it took me a few minutes to release it. This achieved, I made my way to the usual place from which I swam. But it was not as I had known it.

The diving-board seemed to have climbed higher out of the water which no longer sparkled but lay still and muddy in the shallows. Green slime and weeds adhered to the wooden struts which supported the board and a small island in the middle of the pool had heaved its back above the surface like a leviathan. From the whole, murky expanse of water rose a smell of decay. It was not the sweet autumnal smell of dead vegetation but the ugly stench of corruption. One thought of rats, plague, dungeons, sickness. Then I noticed for the first time that a sign-post had been erected on the bank and it bore a notice which said that no bathing was permitted on the order of the County Officer for Health. In just a few days the place had changed from a little lake, tempting, fresh and cool, an oasis of pleasure and relaxation, to this stagnant and forbidding tract of mud and thick polluted water. I turned away and went back to the barbed wire, climbed back into the road, crossed to the van and drove into Berinsfield again.

149

NINE

THEY HAD CONGREGATED on the Green as usual in the early evening, arriving in pairs or threes and fours, with only a single motor-cyclist who propped his machine on the kerb at the edge of the grass and sauntered across to join his friends. I stood back from the window in the shadow of the living-room so that I could see without being seen. I wanted to know the colour of the hair beneath the crash-helmet. If it were long and fair I could reasonably assume that the motor-cyclist was the one who had tried to puncture the tyres of my van, the one I believed to be the vociferous leader of the campaign against me, the principal spokesman and apple-core thrower. If I could get hold of him I was sure I could persuade him to call off hostilities. Neither appeals to reason and humanity, nor grandiloquent threats would have any effect, but a small sample of what he would receive in larger measure if he did not cooperate, followed by the assurance that he, as the leader, would be the one to pay the penalty for any future harassment or inconvenience of any kind caused by him or his followers would put a stop to the war.

Once I had him in the flat I would slap him, open-handed but hard, a single clip just to let him know that I was not averse to such crude means of self-expression. What followed would depend on his reaction to the slap. If he retaliated I would be ready for him. If he tried to use his feet or any of the karate crap he had seen on television I would be pleased to accommodate him. I would knock the living daylights out of the bastard. I would flatten the loud-mouthed, slobbering, ignorant shit.

I was suddenly aware of my hands clenched into white-knuckled fists, that I was breathing quickly and my skin prickl-ed with sweat. I was shocked. Involuntarily I had been creating a fantasy in which my own aggression and blind need for vengeance were allowed full rein, and I had found it exciting. I left the window and went into the kitchen and sat down at the table. My God, this would not do. My mind was rotting in this place. I, who had always professed to despise the hanging and flogging brigade, who was quick to spot the hypocritical rationalization of sadistic impulses in choleric disciplinarians, I was actually relishing the thought of getting my hands on the

youth and brutally thrashing him. If I met Brendan that even-
ing as we had arranged and we were successful in luring the boy
into a trap the fantasy would harden into fact: flesh would be
bruised and split; there would be cries of pain and pleas for
mercy; blood would be spilled. This must not happen. Nothing
could justify it. I would leave straight away, go into Oxford,
spend the evening with my friends, Joe and Polly, and make
sure I did not return that night until the gang had disbanded. I
made a telephone call to ascertain that my friends would be
there and that I would be welcome. Then I left the flat, got into
the van and drove away.

The youngsters' attention was taken up by preoccupations of
their own as I moved off and I was not spotted until I was
driving past, quite close to them. Then a single voice rose shrilly
and was joined by a dozen others in raucous concert. I could see
them, rapidly growing smaller in the driving-mirror, shaking
their fists, jumping about, stabbing V-shaped spreads of fingers
in the air as their quarry escaped them and again I felt the fever
of hatred rising in me. I was shaken by an atavistic need to hurt
them and, briefly, I was tempted to turn back, but the temp-
tation was quickly squashed and I drove on and in a very few
minutes began to feel the relief of escape.

That evening I told my friends a little of what had been
happening.

'Aren't you scared?' said Polly. 'They can be very nasty, kids
like that. And they're not children. They can be dangerous.'

Fear was, of course, an element in the complex of feelings
that troubled me but the fear itself was made up of ambivalent
responses. The simple fear of being hurt was not strong enough
to be of decisive importance. This may sound a foolishly boast-
ful statement but I am as sure as I can be of its truth. Because of
years of training and practice in the boxing-ring I had
developed not only certain defensive and aggresive skills but a
degree of confidence in those skills that, however misplaced,
rendered me almost impervious to anxiety about the outcome of
physical confrontation with an adversary. As my friends were
quick to point out, my boxing days were long past; I was no
longer young, strong and fit; my reflexes would be much slower
than once they had been; I drank and smoked heavily; in short,
I was probably incapable of boxing chocolates. A muscular
eighteen-year-old would make mincemeat of me.

151

I could recognize the force of these objections but my obstinate confidence was unshaken, and it was not entirely irrational. The fact is that a thoroughly experienced boxer – a good-class amateur or almost any class of professional – has learnt things that are never unlearnt. Age, lack of training and practice, physical self-indulgence will slow him down and obviously make him less formidable than he was in his active days, but he will still move faster, with more deceptive cunning and purpose, will hit harder and more effectively than anyone who has never been through the same schooling and, furthermore, the prospect of being hit, which most reasonable non-pugilists regard with abhorrence, causes him very little anxiety indeed. When you are, or have been, proficient in the practice of an activity which the uninitiated will regard as fearsome, it will hold few fears for you: the experienced climber is not afraid of heights, the racing-driver of speed, the swimmer of deep water, the cricketer of the hard ball, and so on. The experienced fighter is not afraid of being hurt.

When I said I was not afraid of my young enemies in the sense of being afraid to meet them in physical combat I spoke the truth as I knew it. And, had there been any vestigial fear of that kind left in me, it would have been swamped by the rage their attentions had generated, for perfect anger casteth out fear. Nevertheless, fear was an ingredient in the powerful emotional brew that was fermenting inside me and it was of a kind that I found more distressing and shameful than ever I could have have found an instinctive shrinking from the threat of physical injury. First, there was the fear of my own lack of control, of the overwhelming intensity of my hatred and, second – and it was this that I found most humiliating – there was the fear of my being made to look ludicrous, pathetic, absurd, and, connected to this, was another, more insidious dread: a terrible lack of certainty about my own strength to resist ways of evading such humiliation, a sickening knowledge that there was little I would not do to appease my enemies; hating them as I did, I would nonetheless seize the chance of ingratiating myself with them at almost any cost of forfeited integrity. And knowing this made me hate them the more.

I spent the night in Oxford and the next day returned to Berinsfield feeling that discussion with sympathetic people about the situation had been helpful. What I must do, we had agreed, was somehow achieve detachment. Polly had said, 'They're behaving like a pack of stray dogs. Don't kick out at them. That'll only make them savage. Avoid them as much as you can and, if you have to go near them, get past as quickly as you can.'

It was probably sound advice, but it was not easy to put into practice. For they were not dogs. They sometimes howled and yelped like animals but, at other times, words were used. You might say that the words were no more than snarls, verbal snapping, they were still behaving like dogs, but I thought otherwise. They were using the language of hatred, of a contempt and loathing so deep that only those brutal monosyllables could convey something of bitterness. But why? I asked myself, why such passionate antipathy? And sometimes, in moments of loneliness, sleepless in the early hours of the morning, I would see the answer shaping itself inexorably: 'Because you are everything they say you are – useless, phoney, soft and idle.'

Then, as the days went by with no relaxing of the persecution, the inevitable storm of cat-calls, obscenities and the chant of my name followed by the obloquious 'Poet!' that greeted my every appearance on the street, the window-banging and the midnight deliveries of insults through my letter-box, I became sick with anger and a kind of indignation that was tainted by self-pity. I lusted for revenge. I stopped going to the pub in the evenings because I could not face running the gauntlet of mockery and abuse. During the day, when the youngsters were not in the village, I would buy a supply of beer and wine, and at night I would sit in the gathering darkness, playing my cassettes very quietly, drinking and listening to the gang on the Green. I had taken to parking my van in a space at the back of the flats in the hope that its absence and the dark windows would lead the gang to believe that I had gone away.

It was then that it occurred to me that I was tasting, in a very diluted form, of course, something of what it must be like to be a member of a persecuted minority group, a Jew in an anti-semitic society, a black among white racists, emasculated, humiliated, constantly threatened, never for a moment un-aware of being different, picked on, unjustly blamed, un-wanted; and this realization helped me to see my situation a little more clearly and brought with it a stab of shame for my lack of fortitude. Millions of people, young children, old men and women, mothers and fathers of infants born to slavery or torture, they had all endured real persecution with infinitely more courage and stoicism than I could whip up to face what was relatively a mildly unpleasant set of circumstances which would disappear with my departure in a month's time when my period of residence in Berinsfield came to an end. I had, somehow, allowed the whole business to become ridiculously inflated.

But the salutary effect of such self-reproaches and strictures did not last for long and my resentment and reciprocal hatred steadily grew until it possessed me to the exclusion of almost all other things. Finally I decided not to be intimidated any longer by the gang of youths and to go on with my life as if they were not there. So, for the first time in almost a week, I went out in the evening to visit The Berinsfield Arms. As soon as I appeared in the road an enormous din arose from the Green. It seemed that their rest from choral abuse had immeasurably strengthened their voices. The uproar was startling, and if I myself had not been its target, I would no doubt have found it comical. But fear and hatred have no sense of humour. I could not prevent myself from hurrying my pace and I was glad to reach the refuge of the saloon bar, though even there I could still hear them plainly and the hubbub did not die down for almost half an hour.

Brendan was not in the pub that evening though Jack called in for an hour or so. I stayed until closing time and was among the very last to leave. I crossed the road, walking quickly, and had almost reached the entrance to the flats before the single voice boomed out of the darkness: '*Scann*-ell! *Po*-et! *Scann*-ell! Knock-kneed old fucker!'

I let myself into the flat, switched on the lights in the kitchen and living-room, and immediately slipped back into the dark vestibule. I left the door of my flat off the latch but I pulled it flush to the frame so that it looked as if it was properly shut. If he came now to shout things through the letter-box I would bundle him forward into the flat, slam and lock the door behind us and then I would have him. I crouched under the stairs in sight of my door and waited. I was tense with excitement, afraid, yet even more afraid of being cheated. The adrenalin was working overtime. My stomach muscles ached with strain

154

and I wanted to piss. Then, through the humming of nerves and pounding of heart I thought, not without petulance, 'I'm *not* knock-kneed. Why knock-kneed, for Christ's sake?'

The I heard a sound from outside, on the pavement. I crouched, fists clenched, finger-nails digging into the palms of my hands, throat tight and sweat starting from my forehead. There was a mutter of unintelligible words and then a flutter of laughter, a woman's voice, mock-reproachful, flirtatious perhaps. It was Mrs Fitzgerald and her gentleman friend returning from an evening on the town. I waited until they had let themselves into her flat and then went into my own and hurried to the bathroom.

'To hell with it,' I thought, 'I'm going to bed.'

My chief persecutor did pay me a visit that night but not until I was asleep when the usual banging on the window brought me reluctantly to a state of semi-wakefulness. I do not know whether or not he shouted through the letter-box because I drifted back into oblivion as soon as, if not before the window tattoo ended. The next morning, a Friday, I went to London where I stayed until Monday morning when I had to return because I was to give a reading at Exeter College to the members of an International Graduate Summer School. I spent that night in Oxford and went back to Berinsfield on the Tuesday afternoon.

I noticed, as I drove from the main road into the village, that while the prison-camp aspect of the place was in no way changed and the surfaces of the roads and patches of turf looked, if anything, drier and dustier than when I had last seen them, I felt less heavily oppressed than usual, and even the sight of the Green with all its attendant associations did not fill me with the customary sense of hunted foreboding. Perhaps that last night, when I had waited fruitlessly in the vestibule and, finally, when the assault on the windows had failed to provoke me to leap from my bed, had been a sort of climax and now the pressure would be eased. For whatever reason I felt less apprehensive, but subsequent events proved that optimism was misplaced; there was no cessation or modification of hostilities; on the contrary they continued even more venomously.

On July 23rd, a Friday, I was to give a lecture on Contem-

155

porary English Poetry to an audience of foreign teachers of English who were attending a Summer Course at Somerville College. My talk was arranged for eleven in the morning. I drove to Oxford, arriving at the college in time for a cup of coffee before the lecture. I stayed for lunch and, later in the afternoon, called on Joe and Polly who suggested that I should stay to dinner and spend the night with them rather than go through another nocturnal skirmish with the Berinsfield Boys. The next morning the invitation was extended to cover the whole weekend but, though the prospect was very tempting, I decided that I ought to go back in case there were telephone calls or correspondence to deal with.

As I was letting myself into the flat shortly before noon I heard quickly-descending footsteps on the stairs and Tony, the AA patrolman, called out, 'Just a minute!'

I paused with the door half open.

He came into view. 'Thought I'd better tell you. I caught a couple of youngsters trying to get into your flat. Just after I got back from work yesterday, about six o'clock. You'd left the little top window open in your bedroom and one of them was on the sill trying to get his arm inside so he could get at the latch for the big one. I told them to clear off and I'd be on the look-out and if there was any more nonsense I'd get the police.'

I thanked him and asked him if he knew either of the boys.

'No, can't say I knew who they were. But then I don't know many people in the village though we've been here over eight years. We like to keep ourselves to ourselves. I expect I've seen them around but I wouldn't have a clue about their names.'

'What did they look like?'

'Oh, you know, same as all the young blokes these days. Long hair. Jeans.'

'Dark or fair?

'One of them was fair, the taller one. The other was sort of mousy. It was the fair one that gave me a bit of lip. Cheeky young bugger. No harm in 'em really, I suppose, but you want to make sure your windows are all shut next time you go out.'

I promised him that I would check carefully and thanked him again. Inside the flat I looked round at the disorder of papers and books in the living-room. There was not much else to excite the destructive impulses of vandals. I thought of Mrs Fitzgerald's report of the desecration of the church and I guessed that, if the youths had been able to force an entry, it would have been the books and manuscripts that would have been the first things to suffer, and I felt myself becoming almost as angry as if the violation had actually occurred. Again the now familiar sickness of rage began to seethe inside me and I prowled about the flat cursing and muttering threats, elaborating in imagination scenes of my visiting violent retribution on the one who I had decided was the leader and exemplar of my persecutors. My hatred of him was a poison infecting and distorting all perceptions: I could even taste it. And the knowledge that he was uncovering in me weaknesses from which I had for long been able to avert my gaze until they had almost ceased to exist, intensified my loathing. The boy, ignorant, stupid and vicious, with his clumsy, oafish bullying and baiting, had contrived to strip me of any vestige that I believed I possessed of the human qualities I most prized, of humour, tolerance, kindness, modesty and – yes – courage. He had managed to turn me into a humourless, intolerant, pompous, obsessively vengeful yet dithering old fool; and, worse, he had shown me the murderer in myself.

I went into the bathroom and, from the mirror above the wash basin, my eyes glared at me, reddened and big with outrage. All of the features seemed somehow thickened and coarsened. They had even changed me physically, turned me into the object of contempt and dislike that justified their programme of abuse. Christ, I thought, I've got to take a grip on myself or I shall end up mad and homicidal or suicidal, if there's any difference. The gang's activities were no longer a severe irritant, a serious nuisance; they were, and had been for some time now, a threat to my very existence.

I went into the kitchen and made myself a mug of coffee, sat down, lit a cigarette and told myself that I must come to terms with the boys by conciliation or the threat of legal action, or I must get out of Berinsfield. And, damn it, I ought to be able to solve the problem without resorting to abject flight. I was fifty-four, I had been around, fought in a war, been on the run, done time, mixed with all kinds of people, some of whom would scare these kids to death. I was literate, comparatively intelligent and had been thought a good teacher. How could I allow this youth and his followers, none of them as old as my own elder children, to reduce me to this state of near lunacy, to harass and intimidate, to rob me of all dignity, privacy and peace. And this attempt to invade my home, this last violation, it was too much. By Christ, they had gone too far. I crushed out my cigarette-end and went to the living-room window and saw that the gang had, as usual at the weekend, congregated on the Green. I left the flat and walked towards them.

They were disposed on the turf in various attitudes of relaxation, some squatting, others reclining on stomach or resting on one side, propped up on elbow. As I drew near there was a perceptible bracing, a concentration of attention, though no one seemed actually to alter his position. My pulses were racing and my breath was coming too fast as I came to a halt and stood, looking down at them. I had to make a great effort to keep my voice under control when I spoke.

I said, 'Two of you tried to break into my flat yesterday evening. I don't suppose whoever it was has the guts to own up... No, I didn't think so.' I drew a deep breath. It was important to keep my voice measured, calm. 'Okay, I can't talk to the ones personally so I'll have to say what I've got to say to all of you. You've got to stop this stupid yelling and banging on my windows and the rest of it. I warned you what would happen. I'll knock the daylights out of you, any of you who means to go on being a nuisance.' I was looking from one to another of the group. Most of them stared back impassively but two of them were grinning. One of these had long blond hair. But so had two other members of the gang, one who was resting on bent knee and chewing a matchstick and the other who lay back, leaning on one elbow, his mouth slightly open, eyes blank of expression. I could not be sure which was the leader.

I went on: 'Breaking and entering – or trying to – is something different. That's for the police and I'm going to get on to them and have them keep an eye on my flat at night and on you lot. I've warned you so don't blame me if you get into trouble with the law.' Then, aware of my weakness and folly even as I spoke, I said in a more placatory tone, 'I don't blame you for getting bored in this place. I can see there isn't much for you to do. But let me have a bit of peace. I leave Berinsfield at the end of the month. Let's have a truce till then.' I felt a daft parody of a smile on my face, false as a party mask, and I despised myself for wearing it. They stared at me, guarded, without expression, except for the fair boy whose grin had never left his face. I turn-

158

ed away and started to walk back to the flats.

Under their scrutiny I found it difficult to walk naturally; my movements felt ill co-ordinated, jerky, like a puppet's. I could feel their attention directed at me like searchlights. They were still silent. I had gone about thirty yards and was almost at the edge of the Green when the single, loud and bludgeoning voice that I now knew so well bawled out: 'Silly old shit-bag!' As I swung round something whizzed past my head. I looked over my shoulder to where the missile had landed on the turf and saw that it was a jagged stone. Overwhelming anger surged and flooded through me, pounded a wild drumming in my head, dimmed my vision, thickened in my throat. I charged towards the gang and they rose and scattered as if a bomb had exploded in their midst. Singly or in clusters they were sprinting for safety and, after I had run fifty or sixty yards, I knew that I could not hope to catch any of them. I stopped, panting and choking with wrath and exertion and as my vision cleared I saw that some of them had fled completely while others remained at a safe distance on various parts of the boundary of the Green, standing in small groups or alone, motionlessly and silently watching me.

I slowly turned and walked back to the flat. No one shouted. If someone had done so I doubt if I would have felt anything at all. I went into the flat and slumped onto a chair at the kitchen table and rested my head on my hands. My limbs were trembling and my head ached. All trace of anger had drained away and had been replaced by a deep, unanalyzable unhappiness, a sense of shame and of failure. I grieved profoundly for a lost something, the nature of which I could not define. My sadness was beyond words or tears or groans. It possessed me entirely.

I must have sat there for at least half an hour before, reluctantly and sluggishly, the necessity for action, the instinct for survival, began to make themselves felt. Slowly, moving like an automaton and without any conscious knowledge of having come to a decision, I began to gather my possessions together and carry them out of the flat and throw them into the back of the van. Clothing, sheets, blankets, towels, books, papers, cutlery and china, pots and pans were bundled together. I moved backwards and forwards mechanically, sweating in the heat but never pausing to rest until everything had been loaded. Then I made a perfunctory round of the flat to make sure that I had taken everything that belonged to me. The rooms looked dismal, impoverished, already deserted. There was a sense – almost a smell – of bereavement in the dusty air. I was troubled by a curious reluctance to leave finally, forever, a guilty feeling of dereliction. But there was nothing to stay for. I switched off the main gas and electricity supplies, shut all the windows securely, went out of the building and got into the van. Then I drove out of Berinsfield. The Green was deserted. I saw no one on the streets as I left and, turning onto the main road, I looked back once at where the village lay in the shimmering heat of the afternoon, the roofs of flats and houses looked over by the water-tower, a construct of concrete, steel and stone, achromatic, heartless, forbidding. I knew I would never see it again.